Rocking Horses

Rocking Horses

Marguerite Fawdry

Pollock's Toy Theatres Ltd

Clown from Skelt's toy theatre sheet 'Harlequin and Old Dame Trot'

Acknowledgements
I acknowledge with gratitude Rachel Waller's contribution to this book, not only in writing the chapter attributed
to her but, more broadly, in communicating to me the fruits of her experience over many years as a rocking horse restorer.
My thanks are due also to Mrs Beryl Cubbon for her researches into rocking horse making in the Liverpool area,
to Mr Richard Lines for the loan of his family firm's catalogues; and to Mr Harry Field of Lines Brothers Ltd
for sharing the knowledge gleaned over a lifetime's working for the firm.

It would have been impossible to compile the information and the illustrations for Rocking Horses in
America without the help of the staff of all the Museums listed on page 94. My sincerest thanks are also due to
The Secretaries of the Historical Societies who spent so much time looking through their local records
on my behalf, notably Barbara Austen, New Hampshire HS; Charles Cooney, Milwaukee HS;
Joseph P. Copley, Portsmouth HS; Lucy Eldridge, Bucks County HS; Philip E. Elwert, Vermont HS;
Lois S. Greenwood, Winchenton HS; Evelyn B. Hachey, Leominster HS; Virginia Hayward, Northville, HS;
Gail Kruppa, Torrington HS; Maurice Montgomery, Rock County HS; and Randall Snyder, Lancaster County HS.

I am indebted to Laurie Weitzenkorn of the Index of American Design, to Mary Francis O'Brien of the Boston Public Library
and to the Editor of "Playthings" for allowing Jennifer Brodie access to past records of this publication.

I am grateful to Mr Bernard Barenholtz, Mr John Noble, Mr Henry H. Schlosser and Mr Lawrence Scripps Wilkinson
for all the help they have given me. This work could not have been done without the encouragement of
Mrs Inez McClintock whose seminal book "Toys in America" was the starting ....

Designed by Elizabeth Newnham
Printed by Richard Metcalfe, Bevenden Street, Lon...
ISBN 0 9505588 8 5

Copyright © 1986, 1989 Pollock's Toy Theatres Ltd, 1 Scala St...

First published 1986
Revised edition 1989

Contents

The Rocking Horse Stud Book

Toy horses are perhaps the most widespread and the most ancient playthings to have survived from the distant past. In museum cases we see them lined up: clay and terracotta from Greece, horses on wheels from Egypt, Roman cavalry, mediaeval knights of bronze or lead. We read of hollow wooden horses being sold in the streets of Troy in the year 425 AD; illuminated missals show us small boys dashing around on hobby horses; prints and paintings depict children pushing and pulling horses of all sizes and shapes or simply careering around, cracking their toy whips and driving along a smaller brother or sister they have harnessed with reins of string. Even small babies were, and still are, bounced up and down on their mothers' knees to the tune of 'Ride a cock horse'. The rocking horse, which occupies such a prominent place in our picture of Victorian and Edwardian childhood, has a genealogy as complex as the stud book of any Derby winner, the wooden breed evolving in much the same way as its live counterpart.

The Eohippos or Equus Przhevalsky of the toy world is unquestionably the hobby horse, its past linked with ancient folk rituals, legends and mummers' plays. At first a painted horse's skull on a stick, later a simple wooden figurehead carved in two dimensions only, the hobby horse was a means of playing at being a horse, of acting like a horse.

The carved head of the present-day rocking horse can claim evolutionary links with such rowdy, frolicking hobby horses as Minehead's 'Town Horse' and Derbyshire's 'T'owd Hoss', as well as with their simple country cousins, child-size horses made from sticks cut from the hedgerow. The body of today's rocking horse, however, traces its line of descent from more noble origins.

Hobby Horse (Pollock's Toy Museum)

Inset: 18th century German engraving from Histoire des Jouets by
H. R. d'Allemagne (British Library)

Facing: The Giant Horse from Orlando Hodgson's The Siege of Troy

War Horse to Racehorse

The stallions that carried mediaeval knights to war were strong, sturdy animals capable of bearing a man encased in coat-of-mail or plate armour, as well as the weight of their own protective armour and the richly embroidered trappings which protected it from rust. Thus encumbered they were slow, and had to be walked to the field of battle on a leading rein. There were palfreys and lighter riding horses too, but only the great feudal lords could afford to keep stables full of horses and feed them through the winter. Few people journeyed far from home, and then mainly on foot. Serfs and peasants worked the land like beasts of burden, with only their own strength to help them.

Tilting at the Quintain (MS 264, Bodleian Library)

Right: Dutch 17th century fairground scene (British Library)

Top: A Stalking Horse. Illustration from The Accoutrements of the Riding Horse (Cecil G. Trew)

Facing: Pantaloon and Aldermen, from Skelt's Harlequin and Old Dame Trot

Top: The Duc de Bourbon, 15th century. From The Accoutrements of the Riding Horse (Cecil G. Trew)

A tiny illumination in a 15th century manuscript now in the Bodleian Library, Oxford, reveals another important strain in the rocking horse's ancestry. Two boys are shown pulling a four-wheeled seat very much like the 'horses' used in gymnasiums today: in all probability it was the stand from the castle armoury on which the lord's horse armour and horse cloths were draped when not in use. Obviously this 'clothes horse' could also be used as a stand for practising mounting and vaulting, or as a stalking horse for hunting. In the picture, however, the three boys are playing at tilting at the quintain. The boy on the horse holds a long pole or lance; and with it he will try, as he is pushed along, to dislodge a target swinging from a post. This was, in fact, a form of jousting practice used by knights.

9

From this mediaeval tilting sport there gradually developed a new kind of entertainment. The post carrying the little wooden hoops of the quintain target was erected alongside a platform which could be made to turn slowly; the riders were seated on rudimentary wooden mounts, and as they passed the post they attempted to dislodge with a stick one of the wooden hoops. An early roundabout, in fact; destined to transform itself, over the centuries, into the flamboyant steam-operated fairground machine of the 19th century. The craftsmen who carved the handsome 'gallopers' for these roundabouts were the same, in many cases, as those who made rocking horses or those other descendants of the early mediaeval 'clothes' horse: the life-sized dummy horses to be found in harness- and saddle-makers' shops, or in high-class tailors' establishments.

There is an evolutionary line to be traced, too, in the development of the rockers on which the horse was mounted: here too it is possible to link the changes in shape and function of the live animal with those of its wooden counterpart.

When Edward III's five cannon fired the first shots in the Battle of Crécy in August 1246, a new era of warfare had opened. As the use of artillery increased, so the need for heavy warhorses declined

18th century English roundabout from Sports et Jeux d'Adresse by H. R. d'Allemagne (British Library)

Left: Dobby Horse, carved c. 1860 and subsequently mounted on bow rockers for Frederick Savage's children (The Lynn Museum, King's Lynn)

Facing: Roundabout with Dobby Horse. Engraving from a Frederick Savage catalogue (Norfolk Museums publication)

11

while the demand for faster horses grew – for warfare, for transport, and eventually for racing; and breeding methods were adapted correspondingly.

Wooden horses, too, changed their shape and movement. In the Museum of London an early 17th century survivor is on view. It is made from two almost semi-circular pieces of wood, shaped like the rockers of a cradle and placed side by side with a seat in between. Springing out in front is a carved wooden horse's head on a long, arched neck. There are the remains of two foot-rests, and on one side a wooden holster with a dummy pistol. A very similar horse in the Nordiska Museum, Stockholm, has traces of the mane and tail of horse's hair it once possessed. On other early rocking horses the outlines of a prancing horse were suggested by legs painted or carved on the large, boat-shaped rockers.

In the middle of the 17th century Arabian stallions were imported into England. The thoroughbreds sired by them were six inches taller than earlier ones, they had a longer stride, and they were strong and speedy. Through the next century the countryside was changing: woodland and marsh were reclaimed for pasture, common land was enclosed and sheep and cattle fenced in. Farmers, richer now and more numerous, local squires and landed gentry found time for, and amusement in, jumping the hedges and racing through the fields in pursuit of the inedible fox.

At home their children practised horsemanship on elegant creatures which resembled the hunters and racers in their fathers' stables. By this time the wood between the legs of the rocking horse had been chiselled away and the rockers slimmed down into long, narrow bows.

Scrap sheet published by William West, 1811

Facing: 17th century Rocking Horse (Nordiska Museum, Stockholm)

Inset: 17th century Rocking Horse with pillion seat and dummy pistols in the holsters (Museum of London)

13

14

19th Century: Horses for Courses

Paradoxically, the advent of steam power and the spread of the railways led in the 19th century to an equine population explosion. The trade and traffic fostered by the railways needed more and more horses to carry and distribute goods to and from the railway stations. Wealth increased; more and more people kept horses for pleasure; new trades arose requiring more horses for their development. Heavy shire horses were needed for carting and haulage. Clydesdale and Suffolk Punches, Hunters and Hackneys, Cleveland Bays, Yorkshire coach horses – all had their different, specialised functions; and equally varied in their style and operation were, by now, their nursery counterparts. An ever-growing range of toys modelled on the horse were available: tricycle horses, beech horses, stool horses, gigs, pole horses, rocking horses with additional basket seats on the rockers.

Below: Illustration from G and J Lines' catalogue, 1911

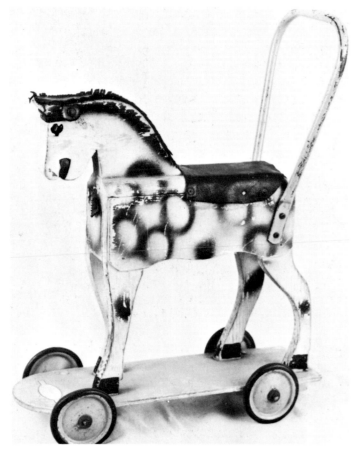

Patterson Edwards 'Leeway' beech horse

Right: Stool Horse. Illustration from G and J Lines' catalogue, 1911

Facing: Illustrations from Wonders of a London Toy Shop
(Victoria and Albert Museum)

'I cannot tell how many rocking horses may be yearly made in London,' said one craftsman interviewed by Henry Mayhew in 1851. 'Perhaps it may be calculated in this way. There are thirty men employed in making rocking horses, and each man can make two a week. That gives 3,120 a year; but as we are employed in making horses of all kinds, as well as rocking horses, you may reduce the number by half. Yes, I think 1,500 may be about the mark.' Over 100 years later, in 1966, Mr George Brown on his retirement from the firm of Patterson Edwards said that he had been making horses by hand for forty-six years, and that he calculated he had made over 35,000 horses during his working life. A vast regiment of Dobbins and Dapple-Greys to be disbursed into nursery homes.

Restlessly swaying, mane and tail flowing, large luminous eyes staring intently, a rocking horse could easily, as he does in Laurence Houseman's mysterious tale *'Rocking Horse Land'*, come to life in the imagination of a child. So too, in Kenneth Grahame's *'Dream Days'* (published in 1899),

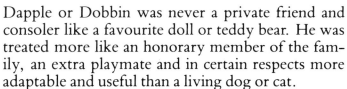

Dapple or Dobbin was never a private friend and consoler like a favourite doll or teddy bear. He was treated more like an honorary member of the family, an extra playmate and in certain respects more adaptable and useful than a living dog or cat.

'Dream Days' is the story of five orphaned children growing up in circumstances very similar to those of Grahame's own parentless childhood. One day, without warning, all the children's toys including a much-loved spotty horse are packed up and sent to a children's hospital.

'In days of old each of us in turn had been jerked thrillingly round the room on his precarious back, had dug our heels into his unyielding sides, and had scratched our hands on the tin-tacks that secured his mane to his stiffly curving neck. Later, with increasing stature, we came to overlook his merits as a beast of burden; but how frankly , how good-naturedly, he had recognized the new conditions, and adapted himself to them without a murmur! When the military spirit was abroad, who so ready to be a squadron of cavalry, a horde of Cossacks, or artillery pounding into position? He had even served, with honour as a gunboat, during a period when naval strategy was the only theme; and no false equine pride ever hindered him from taking the part of a roaring locomotive, earth-shaking, clangorous, annihilating time and space. Really it was no longer clear how life, with its manifold emergencies, was to be carried on at all without a fellow like the spotty horse, ready to step in at critical moments and take up just the part required of him.'

Making a Rocking Horse

General 'Ike' Eisenhower, at the age of 14, used to cross the railroad tracks from his home in Abilene, Kansas, to sand down horses in the C. W. Parker factory. But for most of those who once engaged in the trade the historical record is less clear cut. 18th century trade cards, and 19th century street directories and toy catalogues, give us the names of firms which made rocking horses; but it is not easy to attribute a particular horse to a particular manufacturer, as very few bear their maker's label. We do know how the old horses were made, for Henry Mayhew's informant in 1851 goes on to describe how he set about making a horse:

'The first process is to take a pine plank and form it, by jointing and glueing it, into a block (it used to be made out of solid timber, but the jointing is the better process). The block thus prepared is reduced by the drawing knife and the plane to the shape of the horse's body. It is then what we call bevelled and morticed, to make the holes into which the legs of the horse are placed. The head is shaped out of solid wood (pine), after a pattern cut out of strong pasteboard or thin plank, but we have merely the outline supplied by the pattern: what may be called the anatomy, with the eyes, the nostrils, the skill of the workman being directed altogether by his eye. The legs (of beech) are shaped without pattern, the skill of the workman again having no guide beyond his eye; and the 'tenant' is then cut in the leg – the tenant being a portion of wood left on the top of the leg to be fitted in to the mortice hole made for that end in the body. Next, the head is affixed, being jointed by a great nicety of adjustment to the body of the rocking horse, and then the toy in its rough state is complete.

'After that it is what we call 'worked off' – that is, each part has to be duly shaped, so that all may be in accordance: head, body, legs. Without that there would be no symmetry. The 'working off' is a four-hours' process (taking the average sizes), and very hard work. The first layer of composition is then applied and left to dry, which takes from eight to ten hours. The rasp is next used all over the article, and then another layer of composition is applied, and then a third: this is done to get a smooth, level surface. The last application is rubbed down with glass paper.

'The horse is then painted, and the legs are screwed and fitted to the 'rocker', or frame, which is made before the horse is finished. It is then harnessed – we do the saddler's work ourselves; and after that the mane and tail are affixed. Then the rocking horse is complete, unless glass eyes have to be put in the head, as is often the case.

'We divide the horses into two classes – 'gibbers' and 'racers'.'

At the same time as these details were being given to readers of the *Morning Chronicle* Frederick Savage, an agricultural engineer of King's Lynn, Norfolk, was planning to apply for the first time steam power to the traditional fairground round-about. With the exception of the horses' tails and glass eyes everything was made at the St. Nicholas

Facing: Rocking Horse, c. 1840 (Pollock's Toy Museum)
Below: Carved Work, an illustration from a Frederick Savage catalogue (Norfolk Museums publication)

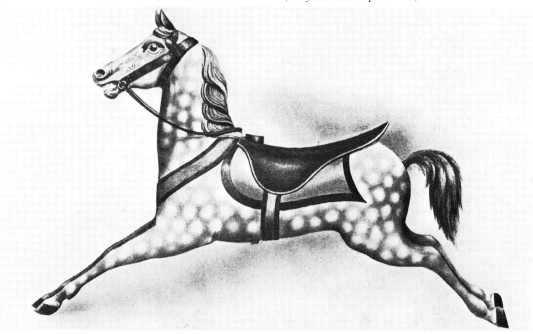

Ironworks; and when these closed down in 1964 all the original patterns and the archives of the firm went to the King's Lynn Museum, together with a charming Hobby horse, transformed from flying horse to nursery companion to the Savage family by being pinned down to a set of rockers.

In 1968 the Museum staff recorded interviews with the last of the firm's employees; and the details they gave of the processes of carving the ornate fairground 'gallopers' are very similar to those noted by Mayhew in connection with rocking horses. Some of them may be helpful to anyone contemplating the renovation or repainting of an old horse.

According to one employee, Mr Walker, 'Knotting was put on knots and blemishes to seal in any grease: this was made up of a kind of shellac and varnish. Small cracks were stopped up with putty, larger holes with a mixture of whitening (burnt chalk) and glue (Scotch glue, boiled up). The horse was then primed with white and red lead; then, in the case of cream horses, three coats of cream lead paint. Early horses were painted in more natural colours: it was only after the 1914 war that the 'straw', i.e. cream colour came in. It was blended up with burnt sienna and raw sienna. For dapple grey horses a white ground was applied and stippled with a sponge with grey. Finally two coats of varnish were brushed on.'

In 1972 Mr Harry Field retired from Lines Brothers but continued making a few rocking horses for private customers.

Harry Field describes the process: it is the process of 1850 still, except in the detail of the finish, 'Years ago they used to paint the horses all over with a thick coat of whitening. When this coat set, it was like a coat of plaster and of course used to cover up the faults, bad joints etc. This was then rubbed down and the spots etc added, and finally a coat of varnish. Now I use a sealer and then a couple of coats of emulsion; and then a coat of lacquer, which is of course more durable. I also found a way of using horse hair, which is more hygienic than the cows' tails which were once used. The tails used to come in large sacks from the slaughterhouse and had to be cleaned before fixing on to the horse. This was not a very pleasant task, for the smell, and then they had to be cured with allum and washed and dried – altogether a nasty job.'

Left: A workshop at 'G and J Lines'
Facing: Lines Brothers' 'Triang' horse, sold by Selfridge's

Designs for Making a Rocking Horse

In his final year at Trent Park College of Education Robert Saunders spent over 300 hours making a large rocking horse based on one he had admired in the Bethnal Green Museum. The periodical 'Woodworker' in August 1974 published an article showing how he had set about his task. We are grateful to the editors for allowing us to reproduce his plans.

'After producing the large profile drawing which included a plan view and sections through the front and rear, there came a stage when no more decisions could be made without starting construction. It was obvious, bearing in mind the size of timber available, that the best method would be to initially make a hollow box and build up around it. It was made smaller than necessary in case of changes that might be made later on. The box was simply made using ⅝″ blockboard. The pieces were butted together and glued and nailed. Pieces of obeche timber were then cut to fit on each end – to give an idea of the overall length. Also, two side pieces were added to give an idea of the plan view. Obeche timber was used throughout for its lightness and because it is easily carved and shaped.

'At this stage I was using glue as little as possible. This was so that individual pieces could be worked on the fairly extensive machinery available in the workshop. Each was fixed on to the box, using dowel rod. I had, by this time, produced all the pieces that made up the body. The legs, head, and neck were made up as separate units as can be seen from the photographs. The head and neck were built up using a similar technique to the one used for the legs. Profiles were cut from plywood, two of each, and separated by using strips of timber to make up boxes approximately 2″ across. Obeche was then used to build up the final shape before carving.

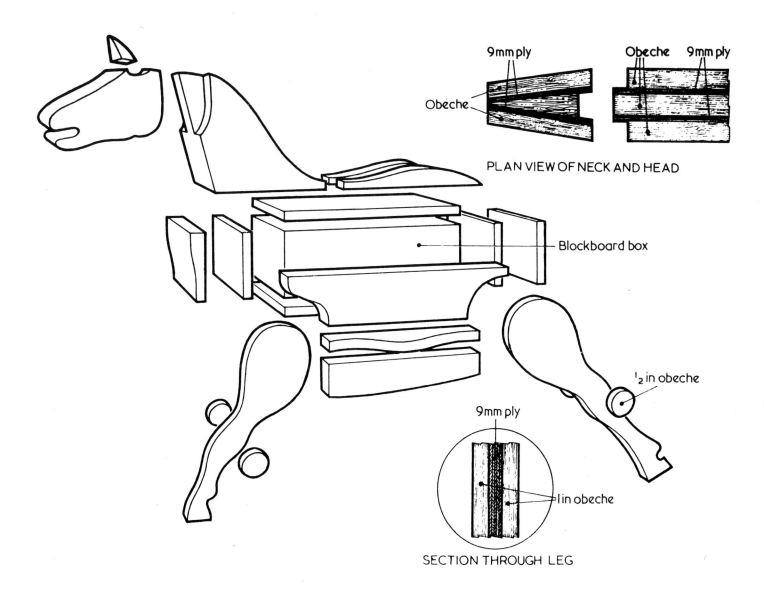

9mm ply

Obeche

Obeche 9mm ply

PLAN VIEW OF NECK AND HEAD

Blockboard box

$\frac{1}{2}$ in obeche

9mm ply

1 in obeche

SECTION THROUGH LEG

'The shaping of the pieces then began in earnest. The equipment used to facilitate this included a circular saw, a bandsaw, a planer and a disc sander. However, I found these tended to be limited in their use and most of the shaping was carried out using a selection of Surform tools, including an attachment for use with a power tool, and a radial sander.

'The legs, body, and neck were shaped almost exclusively with these tools. The head was carved separately; it was mainly trial and error since it was the first piece of carving that I had ever attempted. I used a variety of carving chisels but the most useful were a medium-sized gouge and a large spade chisel. The ears were carved separately and added later.

'The various parts were then all glued together, the horse still not looking quite how it should. I then spent approximately 40 hours using the Surform tools and chisels, only getting the horse to its finished state. The photographs show the horse about halfway through this process. To fill in gaps between the various pieces I used constructional veneer and small pieces of timber. I also used a plastic filler in various places.

'The final finish before painting was achieved both by hand sanding and also a small cabinet sander. Non-toxic paints were used throughout, a leadless primer being followed by four coats of Crown Plus Two 'Scorched Earth'. A set of teeth were next

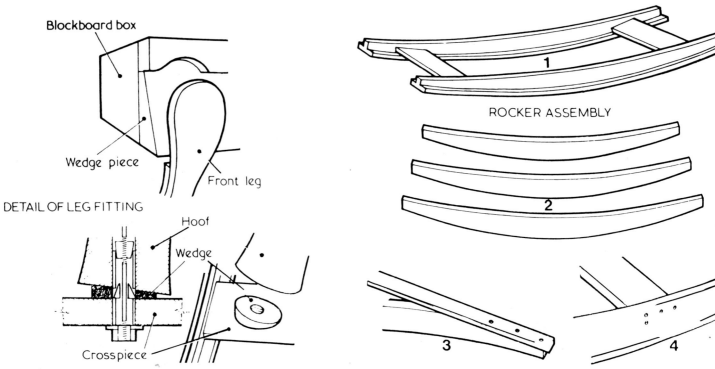

Blockboard box

Wedge piece

Front leg

DETAIL OF LEG FITTING

Hoof

Wedge

Crosspiece

ROCKER ASSEMBLY

1

2

3

4

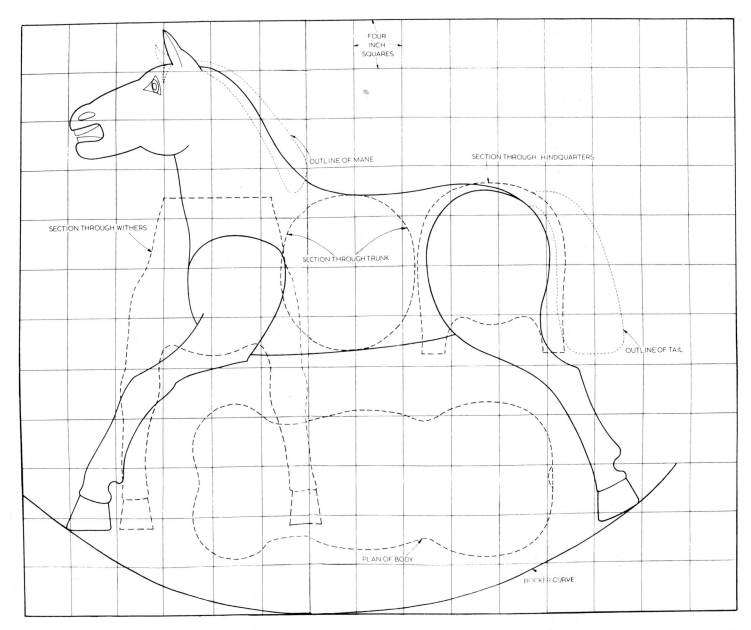

FOUR
INCH
SQUARES

OUTLINE OF MANE

SECTION THROUGH HINDQUARTERS

SECTION THROUGH WITHERS

SECTION THROUGH TRUNK

OUTLINE OF TAIL

PLAN OF BODY

ROCKER CURVE

25

carved, painted and fitted. The paint used here (and also for the eyes) was Humbrol enamel.

'The hair for the mane and tail were bought ready made up from Andrew Booth, a rocking-horse restorer based in Bishops Waltham. The mane is fitted into a slot cut, after painting, with an ⅛″ mortice chisel and the tail is fitted into a ¾″ hole, drilled using a Forstner bit. The saddle and bridle were custom-made for me by the West Essex and Kernow Saddlery in Chingford who provided a quick and enthusiastic service.

'After experimenting with various different curves for the rockers, I arrived at the one I have used. It provides a fairly rapid 'rock' to start with which slows down as the angle gets to the maximum.

'Each rocker is made from a T-section built up from 9mm plywood. First, three pieces of ply were cut to the shape of the upright section and glued together: then two 2″ wide strips (again of ply) were bent around this, fixed by nails and glue. This was then repeated for the other rocker. The cross pieces are made from obeche planed to the angle of the hooves. They rest on the inside lip of the T-section and are fixed via dowels into the vertical rail. The horse is fixed on to these by means of a wedge-bolt system similar to that used in a Rawl-bolt. This gives a firm fixing while also making it possible to remove the horse from the rockers.

'I would like to say, finally, that I am very interested in contacting anyone, either amateur or professional, who is in any way involved in this kind of work. I am also willing to provide any further information about my own rocking horse to anyone who is interested.'

Right: Carving the head of a Kersey Craft horse
Far right: Shaping and blocking a Kersey Craft horse

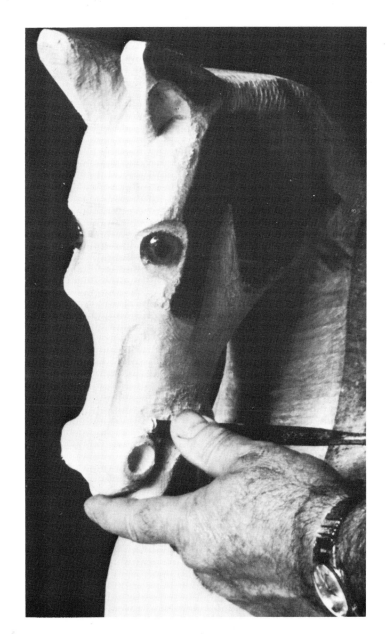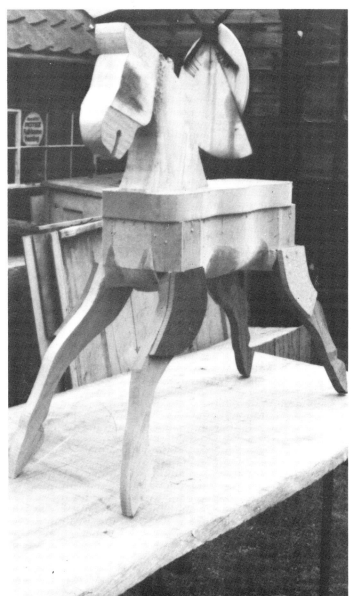

Renovation and Restoration

Before restoration
Facing: A horse restored by Anthony Dew

Renovating a horse is a slow process, and should be spread over a number of warm, summer months.

Before starting, examine the horse carefully for any traces of woodworm. Take several photographs, as close up as possible, and make notes, drawings and patterns of any parts you would like to renew. If the prime purpose of renovating the horse is to enable it to stand up to the rough treatment of small children, then the easiest and cheapest course is to use modern paints and materials. If however, the horse is old and beautifully carved, and is going to be treated with all the care due to a good antique, it is advisable to limit the amount of restoration and as far as possible to use materials similar to those employed in the original construction of the horse.

For many years Rachel Waller worked for Pollock's Toy Museum, restoring toys, dolls and above all rocking horses. Here are some hints from her which may be useful.

1. General Renovation

Mane and Tail: If you are going to repaint, remove the mane and tail and all the fixing pins. They can be washed in washing–up liquid, well rinsed and left to dry in the shade. Refix with panel pins or small nails. The tail is glued in with a small plug: only use wood glue when putting it back.

The body of an old horse is made up like a box, and is hollow inside. It sometimes contains secret items that small children have posted inside through the tail hole: I usually put them back and add a contemporary offering of my own – a small coin, a stamp, a newspaper cutting.

The cheaper manes and tails available today are made from nylon or mohair, though a few suppliers

do have ones made from real horse hair. In the past cows' tails were used as the hair is soft and silky, and curls more gently. If you can get them they will have to be cured: the process is the same as that used for rabbit skins.

Pommel: In Victorian and Edwardian times little girls often rode their ponies and rocking horses side-saddle, and needed a pommel. It is not really needed today, and it makes riding astride uncomfortable.

Saddle and Harness: Old rocking horses do not come in standard sizes. New saddles and tack can be supplied by one or two present-day firms, but they may not fit your horse. A local saddler may be able to help, and to supply you with the narrow leather straps needed for making new tack. This is fixed on with upholstery studs and nails.

Saddlecloth: A strong woollen cloth or an old piece of thick cotton velvet can be used to make a new saddle cloth. As far as possible follow the outline of the original cloth.

Ears: These are often chipped or broken. New ones can be carved from a block of wood, but often a slightly battered ear gives a horse his own particular look and character.

Eyes: Replacement glass eyes are preferable to plastic ones. Before fixing with plastic wood, paint the back of the whites dark red. This gives an interesting glint to the horse's final look.

2. Repainting

(1) Take the horse off its stand and remove harness, mane etc, putting all the bits and pieces in a bag, plus a note for reference. If the horse has a saddle cloth, check the outline and make a pattern for a new one.

(2) If the plaster skin is only slightly damaged, wash the horse in warm water to which a little soda has been added, rinse and dry. Use Instant Polyfilla in thin layers to build up any damaged parts. Do this very gently with the finger tips.

If the horse is in a very distressed condition, all the remains of the plaster have to be removed. If it is dry and crumbly it can be sanded off – but carefully, so as not to lose any details of the carving; if not, cover with several layers of wet newspaper: this will soften the plaster and pull it off as the paper dries. Wetting the horse, however, can cause problems: the wet wood expands, then contracts as it dries out; cracks appear and the joints can start to spring apart. It is essential to leave the horse at least a week to dry out thoroughly. Then fill in any cracks with Polyfilla, and then sandpaper.

When the horse was first made, it would have been given one or two coats of gesso to cover up all defects and then left to dry, often for several months. Gesso is made from whiting and rabbit glue. It was much used on Victorian picture frames, and any book on gilding will give recipes and advice on how to apply it.

A week or so before the horse was delivered to the customer or shop, it was given two or three coats of a lead-based undercoat often several shades darker than its final topcoat. Then, if required, it would be dappled; the ears and mouth would be painted dark red and a touch of red given round the eyes; the hooves painted black; and the whole given one or two coats of varnish.

(3) *Using modern paints:* When the horse is completely dry, well sanded and all the cracks filled with Polyfilla, give it one coat of wood-sealer, then

apply an oil-based undercoat and a topcoat of gloss. If however you have decided to give it a coat of gesso, then only water-based paints should be used, i.e. one or two coats of emulsion, the first coat being a shade darker than the final one.

(4) *Dappling:* Do not attempt dappling until the final coat has had a week or two to dry. Then stick circles of paper or blue tack on the parts you wish to dapple. Then dab lightly round the spots with a stencil brush or a sponge, using a dark grey emulsion paint on your gesso base, or if not using gesso an oil-based paint similar to the one used previously. For the final coat use polyurethane, as the old type of varnish is no longer obtainable.

(5) *Stands:* The stands for the cheaper range of horse were painted in bright colours. Those for more expensive horses were made of polished wood: they can be re-varnished.

3. Pony-Skin Covered Horses
These are very difficult to repair. They are of two types:
(1) The horse is made up of a carved head fixed to a wooden frame, padded out with wood shavings or straw-covered with hessian or sacking. The pony's skin is then sewn on to the padded shape.
(2) The horse has a shaped wooden body on to which the skin has been nailed.

4. Final Recommendations
If at all possible take your horse to one of the firms which supply spare parts, so as to make sure the new accessories fit and suit your horse. Their advice too will be invaluable and willingly given, and save you and your rocking horse a lot of expensive mistakes.

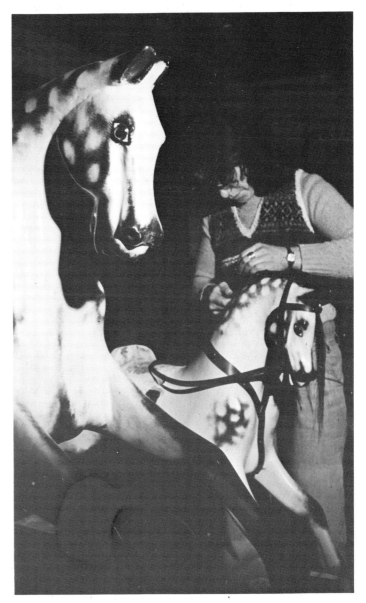

Rachel Waller repairing a rocking horse

Makers and Menders 1989

IAN ARMSTRONG

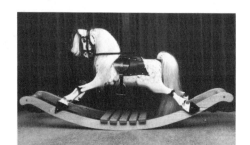

HARRY ANDREWS

ANDREWS, Harry
51 Holly Grove, Fareham, Hants.
Tel: (0329) 237116

Makes hand carved rocking horses with head and body of jelutong wood with legs of beechwood. The larger horses are mounted on safety stands made of Columbian pine, the smaller horses are mounted on bow rockers made from ash. They are all finished with several coats of jesso, painted and dappled. They have glass eyes, real horsehair manes and tails with a leather saddle and bridle.
Also restores and repaints old horses.

ARMSTRONG, Ian
'Sunnydale', North Road,
Hetton-le-Hole, Tyne & Wear.
Tel: (091 526) 4305

Produces three sizes of rocking horses; small, medium & Tudor rocking horse. Will carry out restoration for private customers and supply parts for repair.

BRITWOOD LTD.
Unit B, Martin's Industrial Estate,
Station Road, Theale, Reading RG7 4AE.
Tel: (0734) 303999

Make large rocking horses in ash and nursery rockers in beech with chair back and safety rail.

CAESARCRAFT LTD.
Ryalls Lane, Cambridge,
Gloucestershire GL2 7AT

Caesarcraft design a rocking horse for the younger child which stands approximately 14″ high. The rockers are 36″ long and they come in several colours with hand decoration and harness on them. They are made from modern, man-made fibre of hard and durable quality and a fluffed out sisal tail.

CHESTNUTS
The Oasts, Hurst Farm, Chilham,
Nr. Canterbury, Kent CT4 8DH.
Tel: (0227) 730109

Make traditional wooden horses on pillar stands and bow rockers in plain polished Brazilian mahogany or cedar wood as well as painted dapple grey horses or horses painted in soft pastel shades. Chestnuts also carry out restoration work using only traditional materials. They will also supply a large range of items needed for restoration not only saddles, stirrups, manes and tails etc, but also gesso, glues, antique wax and different types of paint.

CHESTNUTS

COLLINSON & SONS, J.
463 Smithdown Road, Liverpool.

This very old established firm at one time made other wooden toys, today their sole products are dapple grey swing horses made in three sizes. From 1836 to 1850 their horses were painted in different colours. In 1851 Queen Victoria visited the Collinson's workshop and rode a dapple grey horse. Since then, in honour of the royal visit they have only made dapple grey horses. Through family ties

J. Collinson & Sons were related to another Liverpool firm, Baby Carriages Ltd. (1884–1958), who at one time made pale pink and blue rocking horses for Cunard White Star Ltd.

ANTHONY DEW

DEW, Anthony
The Rocking Horse Shop,
Holme Upon Spalding Moor,
York, YD4 4AB
Tel: (0696) 60563

Makes three sizes of rocking horses, undertakes complete restoration and can supply all accessories for the renovation of old horses together with notes and instructions in the use of gesso. Anthony Dew is also the author of *Making Rocking Horses* published by David and Charles (1984) and will supply plans for making several types of rocking horse.

ELIZABETH ELLIS

ELLIS, Elizabeth (Horse Play)
3 Browns Lane, Handbridge,
Chester CH4 7JU.
Tel: (0244) 678322

Specializes in repairing and restoring old horses, using finest quality materials. Also makes a range of miniature horses.

CATHY VAN GOWLER

GOWLER, Cathy Van
84 Kennington Avenue, Bishopston,
Bristol BS7
Tel: (0272) 427765

Restores rocking horses in the traditional manner.

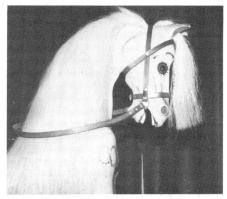

CLIVE GREEN

GREEN, Clive
The Lychgate, 20 Broadmark Lane,
Rustington, West Sussex BN16 2HJ.
Tel: (0903) 786639

Makes two sizes of traditional rocking horses on pillar stands 5ft. or 4ft. long. Lime or an imported hardwood are used for the bodies, beech for the legs and Brazilian mahogany for the stand. The harness and saddles are handmade from quality leather, the horses have glass eyes and the stirrups are nickel plated. Restoration to customers' own horses takes on average six weeks and costs vary between £150 and £300.

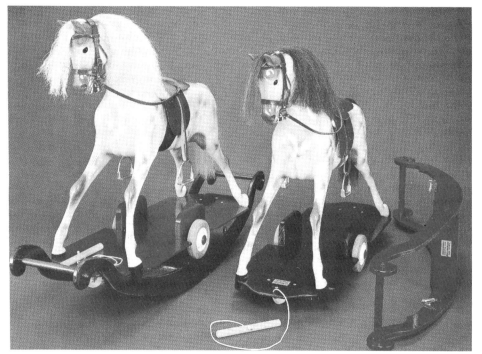

HADDON ROCKING HORSES LTD

HADDON ROCKING HORSES LTD.
Station Road Industrial Estate,
Wallingford, Oxon OXL10 0HX.
Tel: (0491) 36165
Make traditional wooden rocking horses
on pillar stands or bow rockers. School
models: (Special version of the pillar
stand model designed for nursery
schools, hospital etc.) Incorporates a fixed
leather saddle.
Haddon Eventer: Using modern
construction methods and materials but
designed in the style of 1790-1850. Can
be used by one, two or three children at
the same time as a rocking horse or a
see-saw or both.

Haddon Roll-or-Rock: Can be converted
from a pull-along horse to a bow rocker.
Accessories: Haddon-Jeenay safety seat;
saddles bridles; stirrups; mane and tail set
in horsehair including pins and bung; eyes.
Undertake complete restoration of
rocking horses of all ages.

HITCHEM HORSES
Elm Tree Cottage Workshops, Hitchem,
Suffolk.
Tel: (0449) 740211
Makes all types of Victorian rocking
horses in Brazilian mahogany finished
according to customers specifications.
Restores rocking horses.

HODSON, David and Belinda
Golden Dell, Herriard, Basingstoke,
Hants RG25 2PE.
Tel: (025683) 266
Make and renovate rocking horses.

HOLDAM, John
Hen Ysgol, Nantgwyant, Beddgelert,
Gwynedd LL55 4NW.
Tel: (076686) 484
John Holdam's family have made
rocking horses for four generations. His
horses are based on those made by the
Baby Carriage Co. of Liverpool and on
those made by Spooner & Orton of
Burton on Trent. John Holdam will also
make horses to customer's own
specification using glass eyes, horse hair
and good quality saddles and harness.
When required special super-safety
rockers can be fitted. Horses can be
supplied either painted dapple grey or in
polished natural wood.

JOHN HOLDAM

HORSES OF TROY
Caffa Mill, 45 Station Road,
Fowey, Cornwall PL23 LDF.
Tel: (072 683) 3141

Make four sizes of rocking horses, two in laminated hardwood and two in Brazilian mahogany. Horses are only painted by special request. Horses restored in the traditional manner.

HORSES OF TROY

HOUSE OF MARBLES
Broadmeadow, Teignmouth,
South Devon TQ14 8HA.
Tel: (06267) 3534

Dartmoor rocking horses. Individually carved, solid mahogany horse. Real horsehair manes and tails, leather saddles and bridles.
Large size 41″ high, small size 31″ high.
Mounted on pillar stand or bow rocker.
Will carry out restoration.

LABOUCHERE, John
Mill House Farm, North Elham,
Dereham, Norfolk.
Tel: (0362) 81306

Will restore old rocking horses. Will provide parts for saddlery and horses as required including fully cured real horsehair manes and tails.

HOUSE OF MARBLES

LAW, D.J.E. (Woodcraft)
45 Eskdale Road, Telford Estate,
Shrewsbury SY2 5UE.
Tel: (0743) 63845

Makes a simple sturdy plywood horse on a pillar stand suitable for young children aged between 18 months to 5 years old.

D.J.E. LAW

LUDUN DISABLED WORKSHOP
Liscombe Road, Dunstable, Beds.
Tel: (0582) 660261

Make a simple, rocking horse 35″ long in polished beech wood.

MACPHERSON, Stuart & Pam
Ty Isaf, Pont y Gwyddel,
Llanfair T.H., Abergele,
Clwyd LL22 9RA.
Tel: (0745) 79365.

Original horses in limited editions, cast in glassfibre from own models and mounted on wooden rockers e.g. Shetland 'George', Welsh mountain pony, 'Megan', foal 'Dandy', fairground style 'Comet', unicorn 'Orion' (his horn is fitted with a safety swivel device) and miniatures.
Clients' own live horses can be used as models for wooden horses. Authentic restoration work undertaken.

STUART & PAM MACPHERSON

MARRIOTT, John
86 Village Rd, Bromham, Beds MK19 1JG.
Tel: (02302) 3173

Makes individually hand carved wood rocking horses on bow rockers or pillar stands in the style of 19th- and early 20th-century rocking horses to his own designs. Three sizes all strong enough to carry John Marriott who weighs 14 stone. The horses are finished with either a clear varnish or dapple grey paint. Leather saddles and bridles are detachable. Manes and tails are of natural horsehair. He also restores old horses.

MERRYTHOUGHT LTD.
Ironbridge, Telford, Shropshire TF8 7NJ.
Tel: (095245) 3116

Stuffed fur fabric covered rocking horses on metal or wooden bow rockers 30″ high: 'Shirehorse', 'Skewbald', 'Black Bess', donkey called 'Rockie', hobby horses and push-along horses produced in the same designs.

MILL HOUSE DESIGNS
Unit E4, Boston Industrial Centre,
Norfolk Street, Boston,
Lincs PE21 9HG
Tel: (0205) 56585

Will manufacturer rocking horses and child's hobby horses on contract basis.

MULLIS, Robert
55 Berkeley Road, Wroughton,
Swindon, Wilts SN4 9BN.
Tel: (0793) 813583

Makes traditional rocking horses of ash, beech, walnut, oak and mahogany, in five different sizes from 16″ miniature horses to large horses on safety stands 55″ high with real leather saddle and harness, glass eyes and real horse hair and tail. Will undertake restoration of old horses.

PEGASUS OF CREW LTD.
Springfield House, Second Avenue,
Weston Road, Crew,
Cheshire CW1 1BZ.
Tel: (0270) 582131

Rocking horses (covered in washable fur fabric):
Prince de-luxe pony, head height 44″, length 54″. Mounted on a hardwood safety stand.
Dartmoor pony. Same size as Prince but on a smaller pine safety stand.
New Forest Pony. Almost as large as Prince but on smaller pine safety stand.
Shetland pony. Same size and stand as New Forest pony.
Fell pony. Smaller than New Forest and Shetland ponies and mounted on a pine stand.
Welsh pony. Designed for the younger child. Head height 32″, length 35″, mounted on a pine safety stand.
Dale pony. Same size as New Forest and Shetland ponies but with a bow rocker.
Donkey cart. Sit in and drive – steers and pedals. Height 22″, length 39″.
Hobby horse. Length 39″.

PEVERAL ROCKING HORSES
The Street, Hatfield Peveral,
Chelmsford, Essex CM3 2HD.
Tel: (0245) 381 173

The horses are made by Stock Furniture Restorations Ltd. of Brazilian mahogany and can either be french polished or painted dappled grey. Brass fittings throughout, and detachable hand-stitched saddle and bridle. Available on safety stands, the medium and small sizes are also available on traditional bow rocker. Will restore using traditional methods, and can supply parts for repair.

RELKO
Gibraltar Lane, Cookham Dean, Berks.
Tel: (06284) 75605

Rocking horses individually carved from laminated hardwoods, mounted on low bows or pillar stands. All sizes will take any weight including adults. Ragamuffin spring horses: 4′ high based on the Ragamuffin horse produced in 1980 in Guernsey. Will supply separately: saddles, irons, bridle, mane and tail sets and eyes. Will carry out repairs at certain times of the year.

ROBERTS, Roy
King's Horses, 8 Villiers Street,
Hertford, Herts SG13 7BW.
Tel: (0992) 551530/553880

Roy Roberts makes a range of Victorian style rocking horses in moulded "Curanite" with leather saddles and harness and fur fabric covered. "Thelwell's Rocking Ponies" with real horsehair manes and tails.

ROBINSON PARTNERS (LONDON) LTD.
Westfield Works, Charles Street,
Barnes, London SW13.
Tel: (01) 876 7655
Coin-in-the-slot rocking horses. Under the direction of Mr. Holloway, this firm of precision engineers have made coin-in-the-slot rocking horses since 1953. The early horses were all metal and based on a German fairground horse. Today the horses are mostly plastic. They are made in two sizes and can be hired or bought.

RYE, John
Blake House Farm Craft Centre,
Great Saling, Essex CM7 8SH.
Tel: (0371) 2548
Makes handcarved wooden horses based on Victorian and Edwardian originals. Wax polished Brazilian mahogany on pitch pine pillar stand in two sizes, 60" x 46" x 18" and 52" x 43" x 18". Traditional dapple grey painted over gesso on pitch pine safety stand, same sizes as above plus a smaller size 44" x 38" x 16".
Bow rocker models are also available, 84" and 72".

JOHN RYE

John Rye offers a complete repair and restoration service for all rocking horses. Also a range of accessories which include glass eyes, horsehair manes and tails, leather saddles (modern and reproduction), hand stitched bridles and stirrups.
He also repairs roundabout and carousel horses.

SHARNA-TRIANG LTD.
Lumb Mill, Droylsden, Manchester.
Tel: (061) 301 3311
Rocking horses and donkeys for the younger child.
Rocking donkey.
Chestnut rocking horse with casters.
Safety seat rocking donkey with wheels.
Push-along horse.

MARGARET SPENCER

SPENCER, Margaret
Chard Road, Crewkerne,
Somerset TA18 8BA.
Tel: (0460) 72362
Rocking horses on rockers (hand-carved in wood):
Large: 50" high.
Medium: 40" high.
Small: 30" high.

Rocking horses mounted on pillar stands (hand-carved):
Large: 5' 0" long, 50" high.
Medium: 4' 0" long, 43" high.
Small: 3' 6" long, 22" high.
Accessories: horsehair manes and tails, leather harness sets, bridles, stirrups and leather straps, glass and plastic eyes, rosettes.
Will undertake commission work.

STAFFORD, John and Sheila
Dobbin Designs, Otterton Mill,
Nr. Budleigh Salterton, East Devon.
Make hand carved rocking horses in best quality pine or jelutong in the traditional Victorian style, painted dapple grey: other colours on request. Manes and tails of natural horse hair and saddles and bridles of real leather. Stirrups are adjustable. Available either on hardwood rockers or mounted on a stand made from pine or hardwood. They also make fairground style horses elaborately carved and painted, with carved mane and tail and mounted on painted rockers.

JOHN & SHEILA STAFFORD

37

STEVENSON BROTHERS
The Workshop, Ashford Road,
Bethersden, Ashford, Kent TN26 3AP.
Tel: (0233) 83263

Makers and restorers of rocking horses
and carousel horses.

Made to order in traditional designs,
available in dapple grey, mahogany, pine
and walnut. Available in four sizes –
miniature (2/5ths scale) medium, full-
sized and extra large – on Victorian safety
stands or Georgian bow rockers.

Stevenson Brothers delight in
commissions for customers own designs.
They have a large restoration department
and will collect restoration work free of
charge.

Stevenson Brothers have a London
showroom at The Endell Street Place,
Covent Garden (27-29 Endell Street),
where on Thursday and Saturday visitors
can see carving demonstrations.

STEVENSON BROTHERS

THOMPSON, Ian H.
Coalmoss Farm, Ythanbank, Ellon,
Aberdeenshire AB4 0TT.
Tel: (03587) 293

Makes two sizes of hand-carved rocking
horses on pillar stands 5 ft. or 4 ft. long.
The horses have glass eyes, horsehair
manes and tails, leather harness and
saddles. Ian Thompson also makes
rocking cradles, small pieces of furniture,
toys and a simpler plywood cut-out horse
on rockers. He restores customers own
horses and will supply spare parts and
accessories.

IAN H. THOMPSON

VALE, Robert
Bracondale, Hulver Road,
Mutford, Beccles, Suffolk NR34 7UL.
Tel: (0502) 765230

Makes traditional swing rocking horses
on pillar stands and will repair all antique
horses.

WICKSTEED LEISURE
Digby, Kettering, Northants.
Tel: (0536) 517028

Horses for outdoor playgrounds. Since
1920 Charles Wicksteed & Co. Ltd. now
Wicksteed Leisure have been the largest
suppliers of rocking horses for outdoor
playgrounds. The early models were
made of wood with cast iron heads and
tails. The wooden sides were painted
with dappled spots. They could carry
three children. A larger five-seater
version was made in 1950. At that date an
all-steel version was introduced and is still
in production.

WICKSTEED LEISURE

WIFFEN, Trevor
5 Bourne Villas, College Street
Salisbury, Wilts SP1 3AT.
Carved horses made on commission in
natural pine on bow rockers. Each horse
is carved in a different position, as
according to the purchaser's wishes
additional small animals – cats, dogs,
birds – are added. They sit on the
platform, or run between the horse's legs
forming a moving group sculpture.
Trevor Wiffen will also repair limbs and
old horses.

THE WOODEN HORSE
COMPANY
Mansel Kedward, Tam y Bryn,
Brynberian, Crymych, Dyfed SA41
3TM.
Tel: (0239) 79294

Carved wooden horses on bow rockers.
The horses have carved manes and tails
and are brightly painted, more in the
tradition of fairground gallopers than
dappled nursery horses.
Mansel Kedward will undertake
renovations and restorations of traditional
horses and special commissions.

WOODS, John & Dorothy
180 Chorley Road, Westhoughton,
Bolton BL5 3PN.
Tel: (0942) 816246

Make five standard sizes of rocking
horses on safety and bow rockers. The
horses are hand carved and painted in
traditional colours. They also make skin
covered horses, either over a solid
wooden base, or over a straw filled body.
Prices vary from £60 to £250. The cost of
restoration of customers' own horses
usually range from between £100 and
£200. Mr. & Mrs. Woods will also
supply manes, tails, saddles and other
accessories.

THE WOODEN HORSE COMPANY

JOHN & DOROTHY WOODS

TREVOR WIFFEN

Two Hundred Years of Rocking Horses

Rocking horses were made in many continental European countries as well as in Britain and the USA. As they were heavy and expensive to transport, however, it is likely that the old carved wooden horses which have seen service until today were either made locally or by one of the few large firms which specialised in all kinds of strong wooden toys. Very few horses bear a maker's name or label, and many have been repainted or refurbished; so it is not easy to attribute them to particular manufacturers.

In general, early 19th century horses were fixed to steep bow rockers. They were rather narrow,

Combination Rocker and Wheel Horse, from G and J Lines' catalogue, 1911

Facing, left to right: Old-style rocking horse by Lines Brothers Ltd (Triang Toys). Illustration from their 1939-40 catalogue

Improved Safety Rocker with end seats. 'Thistle' brand no. 39. From G and J Lines' catalogue, 1911

'Shaggy Rocker' by Lines Brothers Ltd (Triang Toys). From their 1939-40 catalogue

Head and Chair rocking horse, 'Thistle' brand. From G and J Lines' catalogue, 1911

'Micky' old-style rocker. Lines Brothers Ltd (Triang Toys). From their 1939-40 catalogue

Old-style 'Thistle' brand rocking horse no. 41. Illustration from the last G and J Lines' catalogue, c. 1929.

often painted with large, irregular spots, and had their heads down in a racing position.

Swing safety rockers were introduced from America soon after 1880. The turnings on the support pillars vary somewhat from one make to another; and there are variations too in the shape of the parallel bars and in the way the swing irons are attached.

One particular stable is well documented: that of G. & J. Lines (1850-1931). Many of their horses carried their trademark: a thin metal disc stamped with a thistle. Their horses were sold by Gamage's, Hamley's, and Selfridge's. At the end of World War I the three sons of Mr George Lines set up a second enterprise, Lines Brothers (1919-1972): their horses are marked Triang or Triangtois and were made in the traditional manner, not only in their large British factories, but also in their Australian and Canadian subsidiaries.

Several employees who had received their training at Lines Brothers subsequently set up on their own, making horses which bore a family resemblance; but the horses made today by the successors of this very old firm, Sharna-Triang, are of metal and stuffed fabric. Here is a list with illustrations of horses and their makers of the last 200 years:

1784 GABRIEL, William.
9 Ward's Court, Goswell Street,
London.
Produced rocking horses.

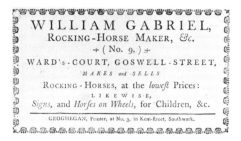

Early 19th century KAIN (late Jones)
25 Ludgate Street, London.
Produced rocking horses.

1822 ALLISON, John
17 Charlotte Terrace,
New Cut, London.
Produced rocking horses.

1822 PALMER, Stephen
26 Hackney Road, London.
Produced rocking horses.

1822 TAYLOR, John & James
2 Shoemaker's Row,
Blackfriars, London.
Produced rocking horses.

1838 ALLEN, John
3 Clarence Place, Hackney, London.
Produced rocking horses.

1838 CARLTON, Richard
6 Webber Street, New Cut, London.
Produced rocking horses.

1838 PALSER, Samuel
30 Webber Row,
Waterloo Road, London.
Produced rocking horses.

1850–1931 LINES, G & J
Bagnigge Wells, King's Cross, London.
Trade Mark: Thistle (Reg. 1910)
Firm founded by brothers George and
Joseph Lines. Joseph retired in 1900 and
his place was taken by George's eldest
son Joseph.
Produced rocking horses 'gallopers and
ostriches' for fairground rides, life size
dummy horses for tailors and saddlers,
horses' heads for pubs and shops,
tricycle horses, stool horses, pole horses,
horse and carts and other large wooden
toys.
Earlier models of wheeled toys had
wooden wheels, later models metal
wheels made in Birmingham.
In 1914 the five ramshackle and scattered
workshops occupied by G. & J. Lines
replaced by one large factory at
Tottenham. Mr G. Lines' three younger
sons set up their own factory in the Old
Kent Road in 1919. Their Trade name:
Triangtois and later Triang (1927).

*'Jubilee Safety Rocking Horse', from
G & J Lines' catalogue, 1911*

'Sportiboy' No. 3, Medieval Tournament Trappings,
from Lines Brothers Ltd (Triang Toys) catalogue 1925

1864–1940 AYRES, Frederick Henry
111 Aldersgate Street, London.

Manufacturer of rocking horses and high class sports goods and board games. In 1887 produced their first tricycle horse. In 1916, they filed patent No. 18070 for a new type of rocking horse, actioned by springs attached to a pillar stand (*see Patents*). In 1940 company acquired by William Sykes Ltd, and reformed under new name F. H. Ayres Athletic Co.

1875 BRASSINGTON & COOKE
Cable Street, Manchester.

Manufacturers of swing, rocking and tricycle horses, wagons and mail carts. Early publicity for this firm states that they were the sole manufacturers of 'Gadds Patent Reversible Handle Perambulator'.
'Swing horses' are first mentioned in 1932 advertisements.

1880 WILSON & SON LTD
Silver Cross Works, Leeds.

Manufacturers of rocking horses, stool horses, prams and carts.

WILSON & SON LTD

1884–1958 BABY CARRIAGES LTD
165/167 Duke Street, Liverpool.

Manufacturers of rocking horses, dolls' carriages, toy horses and carts. This firm also made large horses for riding schools, animal chairs for children's hairdressing saloons, perambulators and tradesmen's vans. In addition they undertook coach painting.

1886 SMITH, J. R. & T.
96 Downham Road,
Kingsland, London.

Firm founded by Thomas Smith, beech horses, carts and engines. Ran into financial difficulties in 1916 and were declared bankrupt, but some assets were salvaged and Thomas's son J. R. Smith, formed a new company, but their factory was destroyed in the London Blitz. Thomas's grandson Eric Smith, with his war gratuity started making dolls and eventually registered the trademark 'Rosebud'.

J. R. & T. SMITH

1890–1929 LUCKETT, & SONS, Thomas
Mark Lane, Petershore, Birmingham.

Manufacturers of rocking horses, pole horses, perambulator bodies and bamboo furniture.

1890 NORTON & BAKER
Victory Works, Horse Fair,
Birmingham

In 1925 manufactured rocking horses 'Wonder' and 'Nib' and tricycle horses, pedal cars, tricycles and juvenile cycles.

1890 SPOONER, Charles John
Swan Works, Meadow Road,
Trent Bridge, Burton-on-Trent.

Designer and carver of waggons, showfronts, and a large menagerie of animals for fairground roundabouts. Also made two types of dappled rocking horses on safety rockers and two types of push horses.

1892 PATTERSON EDWARDS
Old Kent Road, London.

Trademark: Leeway (Reg. 1955)
Firm founded by H. S. Jarvis, manufacturing wooden engines and wheelbarrows. Moved to premises in Peckham station. Their range of toys was increased and included rocking horses, prams, tricycles, coasters and little cars. In 1922 the firm moved to a larger factory in Lee, London SE13, and the son of the founder, Donald S. Jarvis took over management.
In 1955 the trademark Leeway was adopted for rocking horses and prams. The factory was enlarged in 1961 and in 1975 the firm moved to Manor Works, Cray Avenue, St. Mary Cray,

Orpington and commenced to produce a range of plastic toys. In 1966 Mr George Brown, on retirement after working 46 years with the firm said in an interview that he had made 35,000 horses, about 800 each year – the horses sold at £25.19s.6d each.

PATTERSON EDWARDS

1895   DAVIES & CO., Alfred
Penn Road Works, Caledonian Road, Holloway, London N7.
Manufactured safety rocking horses, push-along horses, wagons, cars and lorries. In 1923 changed their name to New Alfred Davies Toy Co.

ALFRED DAVIES & CO

1908   STAR MANUFACTURING CO.

Davis Street, Cubbitt Town, London.
Firm founded in 1887 to manufacture baby carriages and dolls' prams. In 1908 they expanded their range to include rocking horses, swing horses, tricycles, toy motor cars and dolls' houses. In 1915 the trademark 'Swan' was adopted. In 1917 the firm changed its name to Star Toy Co. and added miniature ships and soft toys to its range.
Their range of horses included stool horses on casters, push and pole horses, rocking horses, tricycle horses, cart horses and bicycle horses.

1909   MIDLAND TENT & STRONG TOY CO.
Imperial Works, 129 Duddeston Mill Road, Birmingham.
Manufacturers of rocking horses and horse and carts.

1909   USHER & CO LTD, J
4/Back Guildford Street, Everton Road, Liverpool.
Made rocking horses, push and pull horses, toy wooden sand carts and barrows, dolls' prams and wooden engines.

1912-1932   FRANKE, Bertram E. Jones
London Works, Wellesley Street, Hockley, Birmingham.
Manufacturers of rocking horses and tricycle horses.

1914   HONEY & CO., James
Beckenham Road, Penge, London SE.
Manufacturers of wooden horses and carts, bicycles and prams.

1915   FRYLAND
165 Sherlock Street, Birmingham.
Manufacturer of rocking horses, tricycles and wheelbarrows.

1915-1926   SCOTT & WALKER LTD
Birmingham.
Manufacturers of wooden rocking horses, horse and carts, tip carts, motor cars and a foot-cycle called a 'Skicycle'.

1915 SHILLELAGH WOOD INDUSTRIES
Shillelagh, Ireland.
Firm founded by a Mr Hunter to make rocking horses of Shillelagh oak. In 1919 a new enterprise was set up for Congested District Board to produce rocking horses.

SHILLELAGH WOOD INDUSTRIES

1916 EDINBURGH TOY FACTORY LTD
121/123 Fountainbridge Road, Edinburgh.
Manufacturers of double rocking horses and stool horses on wheels.

1916 ELITE TOY MANUFACTURING CO.
Salt Street Manningham, Bradford, Yorks.
Manufacturers of rocking horses, dolls' houses, forts, engines, motor cars, vans and trucks.

1916 H. S. HOOPER LTD
54 Great Eastern Street, London EC.
Subsidiary of John Warrillow of Birmingham who made toys for J. Frenkels & Co. In 1917 H. S. Hooper took over J. Frenkel. The rocking horse they made was hung between four pillars joined together to form a rectangle.
They also made toy carts.
The firm was acquired by Chad Valley in 1925.

H. S. HOOPER LTD

1919 VICTOR AVIATION TOY CO.
Type Street, Old Ford, London EC2.
Manufacturers of rocking horses covered in plushette. The horse were fixed to a platform with small wheels, which could be fitted inside the larger bow rockers. By 1922 the firm had changed its name to Victavia Games & Toy Co. and expanded its range to include board games. Later the firm was acquired by John Jaques & Son.

1919 WELSH TOY INDUSTRY
Crwys Bridge, Cardiff.
Agents: Gibbon & Son Ltd, 24 Holborn, London EC1.
Manufacturers of 'We-to' wooden horses, forts and engines. Also produced pole horses, push horses on platform and on rockers and stool horses on platform as well as horse and carts.

1920 AJOY LTD
24 Silk Street, London EC.
Manufacturers of a rocking horse, a pull along cart and a perambulator. The horse had an elaborately shaped saddle cloth, and heavy triangular stirrup irons. The dappling was in large circular patches. Pillars supporting the safety rockers were turned like solid table legs. The company made a big feature of their rocking horses. Also produced pole and push horses, a range of eight horse and carts, scooters etc.

1920 KENDRICK, R. & F. W.
Bedford Street, Loughborough.

Manufacturers of a strange contraption –
a 'New' Riding Horse, recommended by
the medical profession as a 'permanent
source of healthy muscle making, nerve
building, instructive enjoyment.' It
consisted of a seat with a horse's head
fixed to a four wheeled platform with a
long handle to push or pull it along. The
seat was fixed at an angle by means of a
spring and bellows, the child could
bounce up and down.

R. & F.W. KENDRICK

1920 CHINN & McMILLEN
23 St. James Road, Kingston.
Trademark 'Chimac'

Firm founded by two ex-servicemen.
Manufactured rocking horses to a high
standard, scooters, aeroplanes and
cycles.

1920 GALWAY TOY INDUSTRY
Earls Island, Galway, Ireland.

Manufacturers of wooden pole and push
horses, cycle horses, rocking horses and
safety horses, horse and carts, trolley
horses, stool horses.
Director of company, Mr R. Hunter
formerly worked for Shillelagh Wood
Industry.

GALWAY TOY INDUSTRY

**1920 NOVEL TOY
MANUFACTURING CO.**
50a Birch Lane, Longsight, Manchester.
Trademark 'Jonbul'.

Manufacturers of wheeled horses that
could be placed between a set of rockers,
horse and carts, wooden carts and
windmills on wheels. The 'Jonbul'
horse's head had glass eyes and
advertised as unbreakable. They were
produced in five sizes.

1920 VICKERS LTD
Vickers House, Broadway, London.
Trademark 'Darenta'

Produced a horse and cart and rocking
horse.

1921–1970 NORTON & BAKER
Victory Works, Horse Fair,
Birmingham.

Horses on bow and safety rockers, in
1925 manufactured rocking horses
'Wonder' and 'Nib' and tricycle horses,
pedal cars, tricycles and juvenile cycles.
In 1933 firm changed its name to William
Barker and extended their range to
furniture and packing cases.

**1922 DOBBY HORSE
EXPLOITATION SYNDICATE**
38 Parliament Street,
Whitehall, London SW1.

Manufactured a toy horse with a flexible
neck.

**1922 R. H. MANUFACTURING
CO.**
26 Wellington Street, Strand, London.

Manufacturers of 'Roc-o-Long'
patented horse which actually walked.

1924 LIVERPOOL TOY INDUSTRY
6 Soho Street, Liverpool.

High class collection of wooden toys including rocking horses. They had rounded stirrups, straight pillars and no dappling. Produced swing horses, pole horses, pram horses, push horses, combination horses, tricycle horses, stool horses and horse and carts.

LIVERPOOL TOY INDUSTRY

1927 DEAN'S RAG BOOK CO.LTD
London.

This firm was a subsidiary of an 18th century London firm of printers and was established in 1905 to print rag books. In 1927 they launched 'Galloping Gus'. Today, under the name of Dean's Childsplay Toys Ltd they produce a fur fabric horse on metal rockers.

48

1928 METTAMAKE LTD
444 New Chester Road, Rock Ferry, Liverpool.

Manufacturers of wooden rocking horses and a construction toy called 'Mettabuild'.

1930-1938 BASHALL, Betty
8 Queen's Drive, Thames Ditton, Surrey.

Betty Bashall began by making toys in the garage of her house in Thames Ditton. She acquired a large furniture van and fitted it out as a showroom for her toys. Her lines included a self-propelling go-along horse and a small rocking seat on four wheels with a shaped horse's head which moved up and down by means of a large metal spring. She also made hobby horses, rocking boats and a kind of Wendy House she called 'Toydens'.

BETTY BASHALL

1933 WOODROW & CO. LTD, G.
Swallow Works, 683 High Road, Tottenham, London N17.
Trademark 'Swallow'.

Director G. Woodrow spent over 20 years working with G & J Lines. His lines included rocking horses, pedal cars, dolls' prams, beech horses. Also produced a nursery rocker. In 1954 produced a metal rocking seat with shaped horse's head.

1934 STAR YACHT WORKS
Marion Street, Birkenhead.

Firm founded by F. Denge. Manufacturers of strong wooden toys and a spring horse which rocked with the minimum of effort.

STAR YACHT WORKS

1937   WHITEY BROTHERS LTD
Jubilee Place, Leeds and
110 Kew Green, Richmond, Surrey.

This firm, established in Leeds since 1854, produced in 1937 a series of 'Fanfare' toys which included a simplified rocking horse.

1938   MERRYTHOUGHT LTD
Dale End, Iron Bridge, Shropshire.
(Established 1930)

Produced push horses and animals of stuffed fur or plush, with wheels fitted to legs or mounted on a strong frame. Up-to-date versions are still available in most large toy shops.

1938   SYKES & CO. LTD., W.
Horbury, Yorkshire.

Old established sports good manufacturers. In 1938 they started to produce 'Trojan Toys' and a kind of low rocking horse – The Trojan Horse. This was marketed for them by J. K. Farnell. They also took over the firm of Dunham White, who made metal toys and in 1940 they bought the stock, goodwill and trademarks of F. H. Ayres Ltd.

SYKES & CO. LTD

1946   FRYER & CO. (NELSON) LTD
Victory Factories, Nelson, Lancs.
Trademark 'Victory-Nelson'

Manufacturers of wooden toys, rocking horses, forts, garages.

1946-1949   GORDON CRAFTS LTD
Gordon Works, Alder Road,
Poole, Dorset.

Manufacturers of Action Toys. Rocking horses and laminated model yachts. Products distributed by Byrite & Sellmore of Caledonian Road, London N7.

1962   J. K. FARNELL
Alpha Works, Acton Hill, London.

This old established soft toy making firm acquired in 1938 Trojan Toys Ltd who made wooden toys, and Dunham White & Co. Ltd who produced metal toys in 1962. They put on the market a fibreglass horse on metal rockers called 'Alpha Rocker'.

"As Strong as a Horse"

J. K. FARNELL

1962   SELCOL
114 Charing Cross Road, London.

Produced a prancing moulded horse on metal rockers.

SELCOL ROCKING HORSE 75/-

This and 6 more SIT'N'RIDE and ROCKING ITEMS for 1962

SELCOL

1963 KEITH LOWE ENGINEERS LIMITED
Dudley.

This firm produced a series of tubular steel toys which included rocking horses, scooters and pogo sticks marketed under the name 'Kelo' toys. In 1970 Keith Lowe Engineers already part of the Central Manufacturing and Trading Group Ltd, joined forces with Wells Brimtoy Distributors Limited and formed a new company C.M.T. Wells Kelo who still manufacture an up-to-date version of this early tubular horse.

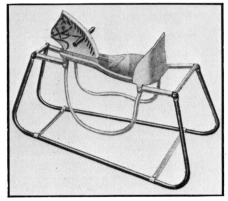

KEITH LOWE ENGINEERS LIMITED

1964 GOODWOOD TOYS
Lavant, Chichester.

Firm founded by Walter Lines on his retirement from Lines Brøs. at the age of 79 to produce strong wooden toys similar to those produced when he was a young man. Initial production included 'Jolly Rockers' and Ski-Rocking horses. In 1973 firm taken over by John Cherry and renamed Goodwood Playthings Ltd. At that date they also merged with Tan-Sad Ltd.

1963 OISIN KELLY
Rocking Horse designed by the Irish sculptor, Oisin Kelly, from Guiness's old oak casks

OISIN KELLY HORSE

1966 PRESTON MANUFACTURING LTD
Manufacturers of a rocking horse on a metal frame and wheeled horses and elephants.

PRESTON MANUFACTURING LTD

1971 KEN BRIGHT & MALCOLM POYNTER
Moving Horse Sculpture.

Ken Bright, a sculptor, who teaches at Goldsmith's College, with the help of a former student, Malcolm Poynter, made first a sample rocking horse for his daughter, then in 1971 a large rocking horse 7½′ high on 12′ rockers, in laminated polished wood. Subsequently, on commission he made two smaller sizes, the smallest size was also cast in fibreglass, and produced by P. J. B. Mouldings Ltd.

1973-1977 COMO ENTERPRISES
Stourbridge, Worcs.

Made fibreglass replicas of Victorian rocking horses. Hand-painted with real horse hair mane and tail on natural pine safety rockers. The horses were made in two sizes – the largest measured 4′ from ground to top of head and was 4′-6′ from rear hoof to head.

1979 THE TROJAN HORSE CO.
Unit 6, King Street Trading Estate, Middlewick, Cheshire CW16.

Fibreglass horse, detachable leather saddle and harness, horsehair mane and tail. Wooden straight rockers, turned pillars. Sold at Heals Ltd.

1976-1981 RAGAMUFFIN TOYS
Feremina, St. Martin's, Guernsey, Channel Islands.

Moulded fibreglass horses mounted on a hardwood frame. The horses move up and down, their movement being controlled by large coil springs. They are 53″ high and 67″ long.

RAGAMUFFIN TOYS LTD

EQUESTRIS

HARRY FIELD

About 200 were made, and sold mainly to Infant Schools in England. One was purchased by the Bethnal Green Museum, London.
Production ceased in 1981, but Mr Harold Briginshaw, who designed this modern version of an older type of rocking horse, still has a stock of horsehair manes and tails, as well as stirrups, suitable for repairs.

1979 EQUESTRIS
79 Maltravers Street, Arundel, Sussex.
Large horse and Shetland pony, soft velvet fabric coat, mounted on safety stands. Sizes 3′ 6″ and 5′ 6″. Push horse – hand painted, birch ply body, mahogany handle.

1922-1979 FIELD, Harry
14 Lidiard Road, Earlsfield, London SW18.
Mr Harry Field worked for Lines Bros. from 1922 until 1973 – making rocking horses. On his retirement he continued to make horses in the traditional manner for a shop, run by Peter Greenhill in Wimbledon called Thingummies. The rocking horses were sold under the label 'Ray Delphi'.

Tricycle Horses, Beech Horses & Other Stable Companions

'The Startler'. G and J Lines' 1911 catalogue

In June 1822, in Paris, Monsieur Combe patented a 'vélocipède' – a pedal tricycle horse. Five months later Monsieur Goudoux patented his 'vélocimane' – a tricycle horse worked by handles in the head. Both toys prospered and were later taken up by a number of Birmingham firms making bicycles or perambulators.

Little children who were too young to ride these tricycles and too small to climb on to a rocking horse had a long-suffering friend, 'Dobbin', who could be pushed and pulled about, and whose back was broad enough to ride on. These simple beech horses had round, barrel-shaped bodies, a horse's head and neck which fitted into a slot as in early 16th century rockers, a real hair tail, and four straight legs which fitted on to a low, wheeled platform. Most also had a handle to push with. Some had leather harnesses; the cheaper ones had red painted reins and strips of blue paper stuck on to represent a saddle. They came in several sizes, the largest being about two feet tall. A number of timber yards and other workshops turned them out as a sideline; other more established firms offered them as a cheaper line alongside their more expensive ranges.

The Tea Garden: engraving after George Morland (Victoria and Albert Museum)

Principal tricycle horse manufacturers

1896-1956 CARTWRIGHT & CO., F. A.
Birmingham.
Manufacturers of 'Rajah' horse trikes.

1908 COLE, T. T.
Sparkbrook, Birmingham.
Manufacturers of cycle horses, push horses and hobby horses.

1913 CARTWRIGHT & WATKINS
10 Bissell Street, Birmingham.
(Offices: 27 Barbican, London EC)
Manufacturers of tricycle horses, pedal cars, tricycles and cycles.

CARTWRIGHT & CO

1915-1930 SPENCER, Lewis
322 Oldham Road, Manchester.
Timber merchant and toy manufacturer. In 1919, the firm was making 'The Victory Glider', a tricycle with horse's head, push bike wheels, no pedals, just foot rest, no steering. Made in three sizes.

1918 McERLAND, D.
51 Bedlay Street, Springburn, Glasgow.
Manufacturers of horse Vélocipèdes.

1918 TOYCRAFT WORKS
26 Little Camden Street, Camden, London NW1.
Manufacturers of 'The Scooter Horse', three wheels and all wood construction.

WOODEN TOYS OF DISTINCTION AND QUALITY

THE "SCOOTER HORSE" SOMETHING WHICH WILL NOT BE SEEN AT THE EXHIBITION

Built in 3 sizes.

Design Registered.

Finished in Enamel Colors.

TOYCRAFT WORKS. 26, LITTLE KING STREET CAMDEN-TOWN N.W.

TOYCRAFT WORKS

1920 TAN-SAD LTD
Freeman Street, Birmingham.
Firm founded by F. H. Headley, a member of a Quaker family, for the manufacture of motor cycle seats. They then progressed to folding scooters and prams and registered the trademark 'Tan-Sad' in 1922.
1927. Produced 'Trisky Trike', a toy horse on one large and two small wheels.
1928. Produced a pedal driven horse with a realistic galloping action 'Tipperary Tim'.
1933. Produced 'The Galloper', an entirely new type of three legged rocking horse which moves forward with a natural realistic action. No mechanical parts to break or get out of order. (*See Patents.*)
1935. Moved to Tipton and amalgamated with Richards, Son & Allwin Ltd, one of the largest manufacturers of prams and scooters.
1958. Produced 'Rocking Dobbin' tubular frame with horse's head.
1974. Tan-Sad merger with Goodwood Playthings.

TAN-SAD LTD

Principal beech and other horse manufacturers

1916   THORP, J & T.
Portugal Street, Manchester.
Wood turners and manufacturers of
wooden horses, horse and carts.

1901-1933   WANKLYN, Alex
17 Manchester Avenue,
Aldersgate Street, London EC.
Manufactured white wood horses.
Street Directories 1901-1933 described
him as a General Merchant. In 1930 was
registered as Wanklyn Ltd.

1908-1915   ASTON LTD, W. H.
Reliance Works, James Street,
Worcester.
Manufacturers of wooden toys, beech
horses, stool horses, hobby horses,
horse and carts, engines, trucks,
barrows, push chairs.

1912   FRAKE, W.
35 Preston Street,
Bethnal Green, London E.
Manufacturers of wooden toys, beech
horses, carts and pole wagons.

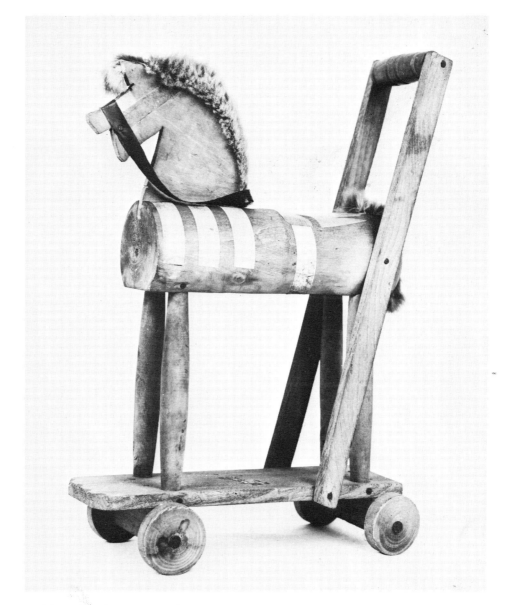

Beech horse (Pollock's Toy Museum)

**1915 LORD ROBERTS'
MEMORIAL WORKSHOPS**
Britannia Road, Fulham, London SW.
Manufactured 'Gee-Whiz-Gee' – stool horse, low seat on four wheels with a shaped horse's head in front. 'Galloping Gee-Gee', a push-along wheel and horse. Also manufactured horse and carts and hobby horses.
In 1920 produced 'The Charger' with life-like movements of head and tail. Very strongly made.

LORD ROBERTS' MEMORIAL WORKSHOPS

1916 KAYE TOY CO.
Lockner Road,
Kingsland Road, London.
Manufacturers of animals on wooden and metal wheels. Beech horses, wheelbarrows and push chairs.

1917 McCAUL'S WATERFORD TOY CO.
Stephen Street and Patrick Street, Waterford.
Offices: 28 Barrow Strand Street, Waterford
Manufacturers of stool horses.

1918 ELLIS & CO. LTD
Prince Street, Newport, Monmouthshire.
Manufactured a wooden stool horse called 'Galloping Gee-Gee' which really galloped and was self-propelled and safe. Also manufactured the 'John Bull' scooter car.

1919 CRITCHLEY HARDWARE CO.
King Street, Stroud, Gloucestershire.
Manufacturers of whip tops, scooters, horses, carts, waggons.

1919 DALSTON BABY CARRIAGE CO. LTD
544 Kingsland Road, London E8.
Manufacturers of beech horses, bath chairs and baby carriages.

1919 DUFFELL, Edward
Empire Works, 41 Morning Lane, London E9.
Manufacturers of hobby horses, horse and carts.

1919 NEWTON & SON LTD
17 Sandgate, Newcastle-upon-Tyne.
120 Quayside, Newcastle-upon-Tyne.
Offices: 110 Leonard Street, London EC.
Manufacturers of children's rockers in various animal shapes, engines, aeroplanes, swing boats and barrows.

1919 RENISONAT LTD
Point Pleasant Wharf,
Putney Bridge Road, London SW18.
Manufacturers of 'Toyzona' horses and carts. One of the Directors was formerly with Lord Roberts' Memorial Workshops.

1920 CHAPMAN & SON LTD, A
2 Jebb Street, Bow, London E.
Manufacturers of beech horses and hobby horses.

1920 DELITE ALL WOOD TOY CO.
Bromfield, Mold, North Wales.
Manufacturers of dappled wood stool horses.

1920 HARRISON, C. P.
Sheffield.
Manufacturers of a bouncing horse, pull-along on four wheels.

1920 ROBERTS & CO., D.
126 St. Ann's Road, Tottenham, London N15.
Manufacturers of wooden horses and carts, brewer's dray, coal cart and luggage cart.

1920 THEAKER BROS.
159 Bromhall Street, Sheffield.
Manufacturers of stool horses and other wooden toys.

1920 TOYS (KIDDERMINSTER) LTD
106 Mill Street, Kidderminster, Worcs.
Manufactured a toy horse and cart. Legs were pivoted which gave a life-like walking action when toy was moved forward.

TOYS (KIDDERMINSTER) LTD

1920 TWEED, H.C.
Cross Road Works, Lexden, Colchester, Essex.
Manufacturers of wooden toys, beech horses, ska cycles, wheelbarrows and 'baby chariot' walker.

1921-1957 BOURNEMOUTH NOVELTY WORKS

St. Paul's Lane, Bournemouth, Dorset.

Manufacturers of 'Sturdi' wooden toys. In 1937 they made a horse 'Come on Steve', based on a Sunday Express cartoon.

BOURNEMOUTH NOVELTY WORKS

1927 POPES

Brockenhurst, Hampshire.

Manufactured 'Stag Brand' beech horses.

1931 MONTIL MANUFACTURING CO.

Britannia Works,
Morville Street, Birmingham.

Produced a 'Gee-gee Kar' and a 'Gee-gee Toddler'.

1932 JOY-TOY CO.

51 Hanley Road, Finsbury Park, London N4.

Wooden toy manufacturers who produced a pull-along horse.

JOY-TOY CO

1935 TWILLEY & ADAMS

65 Chancery Lane, London WC2.

Toy importers, including horses and hay wagons.

TWILLEY & ADAMS

1940 ASHCOURT TOY CO. LTD

76 Worship Street, London EC2.

Produced a hand-made horse and trailer called 'Ashcourt'. Also manufactured wooden pull-along toys, barrows attached to funny animals wearing clothes.

ASHCOURT TOY CO. LTD

1946 DRIVER, Robert

Piccadilly, Manchester.

Manufactured a galloping horse and dray, wooden, moving pivoted legs.

ROBERT DRIVER

1954 REMPLOY TOYS

Oxgate Lane, Cricklewood, London NW2.

Manufactured a single rocking horse seat made of highly polished natural wood.

1965 SEBEL & CO. LTD, D.

West Street, Erith, Kent.

Company founded by D. Sebel for the manufacture of iron railings, fire escapes, wheels for trucks, trolleys and motor cars. After World War II. D. Sebel and his son Harry engaged a sculptor George Morwood to design some large toys for them. 'Mobo Bronco' was a cantering horse. The weight of the child in the saddle caused the legs of the horse to contract pressure on the stirrups, caused the legs to shoot foward and the horse to canter. 'The Spring Horse' was a large horse suspended by springs to a stand.

SEBEL & CO. LTD

1967 MARX LOUIS & CO. LTD

Produced 'Marvel the Mustang' a 25″ high galloping horse activated by strong individual type coil spring.

Skin- and Fur-Fabric Horses

Before and immediately after World War I a great number of rocking horses were imported into England from Germany and Switzerland. These were not carved wooden horses like the traditional English ones, which were heavy and expensive to transport, but cheaper, lighter, mass-produced horses with papier-maché heads and stuffed bodies on a simple wooden frame covered with real skin, or plush or felt.

During the years 1914–1918, when imports of foreign toys were strictly controlled, the foundations of the soft toy industry in England were laid.

A wooden framed horse showing its straw and sacking body before being re-covered with a new pony skin (Rachel Waller restoration, 1976)

Principal manufacturers

1917 ISAACS & CO.
Highgate Park Works,
Alcester Street, Birmingham.
Manufacturers of a large 'walkhorse'
with legs on small wheels.

1919 WHOLESALE TOY CO.
52a Blackstock Road,
Finsbury Park, London N.
(Agent: Cowan de Groot)
Manufacturers of 'Hercules' range of
plush toys on wheels and rocking horses
on wheeled platform, clipping into set of
bow rockers. Handle at back of stand to
push horse or as extra precaution when
used as a rocker.

WHOLESALE TOY CO

1920 STONE & CO., H. G.
New Union Street, London.
H. G. Stone (1873-1934) was a partner in
the soft toy business of J. K. Farnell &
Co. He left in 1920 to found his own
business in conjunction with L. Rees &
Co. In 1924 they registered the brand
name 'Chiltern'
After Mr Stone's death his son carried on

the business and designed for the firm
'Panurge Pets', which included a horse
on wheels with a trotting movement,
and 'Panurge Piebald', a circus horse
covered in mohair plush, strong enough
to take the weight of a man. Also
produced horses, ponies and donkeys
fitted with a steering device.

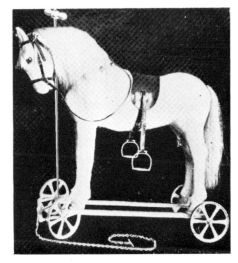

H.G. STONE & CO

**1927 DEAN'S RAG BOOK CO.
LTD**
London.
This firm was a subsidiary of an 18th
century London firm of printers and was
established in 1905 to print rag books
and dolls. In 1927, they launched
'Galloping Gus' the lucky gee-gee.
Today, under the name of Dean's
Childsplay Toys Ltd they produce a
fur-fabric horse on metal rockers.

1938 MERRYTHOUGHT LTD
Dale End, Iron Bridge, Shropshire.
(Established 1930)
Produced push horses and animals with
wheels fitted to legs of stuffed fur or
plush, or mounted on a strong frame.
Up-to-date versions are still available in
most large toy shops.

1946 T. T. INDUSTRIES LTD
Duke Street, Fenton, Stoke-on-Trent,
Staffs.
Produced heavy-gauge wheeled toys
and rocking horses.
Firm founded in 1914, formerly called
Teddy Toy Co.

1968 FARNELL, J. K.
Alpha Works, Acton Hill, London.
This old established soft toy making
firm, acquired in 1938 Trojan Toys Ltd,
who made wooden toys and Dunham
White & Co. Ltd, who produced metal
toys in 1962. They put on the market a
fibreglass horse on metal rockers called
'Alpha Rocker'.

1979 EQUESTRIS
79 Maltravers Street, Arundel, Sussex.
Large horse and Shetland pony, soft
velvet fabric coat, mounted on safety
stands. Sizes 3' 6" and 5' 6". Push horse –
hand painted, birch ply body, mahogany
handle.

British Patents

An advertisement in the *Pennsylvania Packet* for September 10, 1785, states that William Long, a cabinet maker and carver from London, 'respectfully informs the ladies and gentlemen of the city that he makes Rocking Horses, to teach children to ride and give them a wholesome and pleasant exercise.'

Late 18th century and early 19th century horses were, as William Long tells us, made as training devices; and because of this they were carved in a racing position, head and ears lowered, and were mounted on very steep rockers. If the rider did not hang on in the correct manner he was thrown over the horse's head.

Most of these early rockers lived in country estates, where there was ample space to play indoors on a rainy day, and where any damage done to the floor by these large rockers was not of great importance. But once they started to migrate to middle class town houses the wear and tear to carpets and nursery flooring caused trouble, and gave rise during the second half of the century to a number of ingenious inventions.

One of the earliest patents was taken out in England in 1861 by William Kennedy. He envisaged a horse mounted on springs attached to the horse's hooves, on which it would bounce up and down. In America the firm of Crandall made a horse mounted on a huge coiled spring; and in recent years the Guernsey firm, 'Ragamuffin', made glassfibre horses mounted in the same way. By far the most important revolution, however, was heralded by the patent granted to the Cincinnati firm of W. Marqua, who mounted his horses on pillar safety stands. The horses swung to and fro, and there was little danger of a child falling off. This principle was soon adopted in Europe as well as in the USA.

The universal preference for the safety swing stand has not, however, deterred inventors from devising all kinds of ingenious ways of attaching horses to different types of stands, or from making prototypes of horses which could prance about free of either stands or rockers. Here is a small selection from a huge field:

1861 KENNEDY, William
Rocking horse which moved up and down.
Patent No. 578

1912 WILBE, H.
21 Finchley Road, London
Mechanical horse exercising device.
Patent No. 5291

1915 QUINCEY, S.
127 Hainault Avenue, Westcliffe, Essex.
Horse and velocipede. Saddle moves vertically up and down.
Patent No. 15379

1916 AYRES, F. H. LTD
T. R. Freeman, 111 Aldersgate, London.
A support for a rocking horse.
Patent No. 18070

1922 DOBBY HORSE EXPLOITATION SYNDICATE
38 Parliament Street, London SW1.
Horse with 'flexible' neck.
Patent No. 11626

DOBBY HORSE EXPLOITATION SYNDICATE

1922 NOVEL TOY MANUFACTURING CO. LTD
50a Birch Lane, Longsight, Manchester.
Five sizes 'Jonbul' with unbreakable head.
Patent No. 437/22

NOVEL TOY MANUFACTURING CO. LTD

1922 R. H. MANUFACTURING CO.
26 Wellington Street, Strand, London WC2.
'Roc-o-Long' horse which walked.
Patent No. 191209

R. H. MANUFACTURING CO

1923 HONEY, E. T.
9 Tredown Road, Sydenham, London.
Horse supported centrally on a roller or wheels. Four legs pivoted at knee joints.
Patent No. 196,434

1924 READER, L. M.
19 Downs Road, Clapton, London.
and HAYNES, C. A.
4 Birchwood Avenue,
Muswell Hill, London.
Rocking horse, front legs pivoted to body.
Patent No. 206,679

1924 STARK BROS. LTD
and VALE, H. E. T.
1 Church Street, Kensington, London.
Rocking horse on two part triangular
frame.
Patent No. 280,111

1925 EDGAR, E.C.
Staff Quarters, Brompton Barracks,
Chatham, Kent.
Rocking horse and vélocipèdes.
Front and back legs pivoted upper ends.
Horse propelled by weight of rider.
Patent No. 236,670

1925 PRICE, T.
Ship Inn, Church Street,
Llanelly, Carmarthenshire.
A galloping horse, vélocipèdes, legs
move as the body moves.
Patent No. 222,222

1925 CRAWSHAW, A.
Oughtebridge Vicarage, Sheffield.
Folding rocking horse.
Patent No. 231288

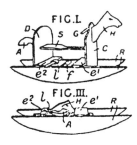

1927 JONES, William Henry
Charterhouse Buildings, London.
'Mournful Mike' toy horse.
Reg. trademark No. 478696.
Patent No. 728081

1933 TAN-SAD LTD
Galloper rocking horse.
Patent No. 380611

TAN-SAD LTD

TROY TOY MANUFACTURING CO. LTD

**1935 TROY TOY
MANUFACTURING CO. LTD**
165/7 Moorgate Street, London EC2.
'Troyhorse', a horse with no pedals, no
mechanism. Could move forward, and
right and left doing 'everything' a real
horse can do except bite'.
Patent No. 94934

1947 WHILEY BROS.
110 Kew Green, Richmond, Surrey.
'Dizzy' and 'Pancho' – the walking
rocking horses. They rock, they walk,
they turn.
Patent applied for 1947

WHILEY BROS

1947 WOGGLE TOYS LTD
Staines Road, Hounslow, Middlesex.
Wonderful walking toys, animals and
people.
Patent No. 609641

*Facing: 'Bronco Buster', a pressed steel horse
mounted on a new type of metal stand.
With soft rubber mane, tail & saddle.
Lines Brothers Ltd (Triang Toys), 1955*

Shooflies Hobby Horses and Velocipedes

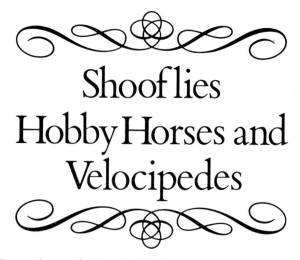

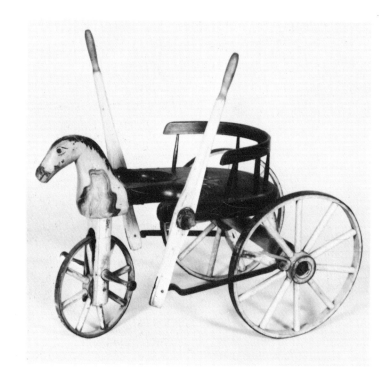

A Question of Vocabulary

Many simple everyday words suffer a sea change crossing the Atlantic. At the beginning of this short account of the History of Rocking Horses in America a clarification of terminology is therefore necessary.

First the term 'Hobby Horse'. For the Pilgrim Fathers, according to erudite sources, a hobby horse was either a small sturdy four-legged animal, or a wanton girl ridden by all and sundry. Later 20th-century American dictionaries give six other definitions: a rocking horse, a favourite subject, a figure of a horse attached to a Morris Dancer, an early form of bicycle, a stick with a horse's head and an imitation horse on a merry-go-round.

Harold Wentworth in his Dictionary of American Slang adds still further ramifications. A "hobby horse" says he, means "a translation as related to a pony". This most obscure phrase is clarified by his definition of 'pony' – as a translation

of a foreign language without the teacher's knowledge; any unethical aid used by a student; a race horse; a burlesque dancer.

To avoid confusion in the following pages no attempt will be made to adopt American spelling or to use American terms so 'rocking horse' and not 'hobby horse'; 'hobby horse' and not 'stick horse'.

There are two other children's toys that were sometimes decorated with horses heads, tricycles and a kind of go-cart operated by hand levers, known respectively in the American toy trade as 'velocipedes' and 'propellers'. In the list of manufacturers we have, however, listed these toys under their American name.

Above: Wooden horse painted black with grey rockers, 19th century (New York Historical Society)

Facing: Rocking horse with padded seat. Could this be the horse made by Woodbury G. Gerrish of Portsmouth? (The Henry Ford Museum, Dearborn)

Top: 19th-century propeller (Essex Institute, Salem)

American Home-bred Horses

A charming water-colour painted by John White who in 1587 became Governor of the First Colony of Virginia, shows a Roanoke Indian girl, naked except for a string of beads, clutching a small wooden doll made in England and dressed in the height of Elizabethan fashion, proof that it was thought expedient to bring a few toys to barter with the indigenous inhabitants of the New World.

During the next two centuries a few toys were imported. Rich travellers also brought back from their travels in Europe more expensive souvenirs. Faced with overwhelming hardships and difficulties the early settlers in America had little money to spend on unnecessary frivolities and not much time to spare making toys for their children. By the 18th and early 19th century life on the farms and in the small towns had become prosperous enough for some devoted fathers or rural craftsmen to make a few simple toys. Among the most touching are the crude rocking horses which have survived.

In the Bucks County Historical Museum at Doyleston, Pennsylvania is a horse very similar to 17th-century horses found in Europe. The body is made of three pieces of hemlock spruce. It has been painted white and then decorated with dark patches formed by smoking it with a candle. A slightly more sophisticated version of this type of horse rocking-seat is in the Henry Ford Museum.

In St. Nicholas Magazine 1870 a little illustration shows another country horse, just a log of wood, a crude head and four stick legs mounted on a simple rocker that could have been made in a few hours by a devoted father or a rural craftsmen.

Above: Wooden rocking horse made c. 1850 by Jonathan A. Kenny for his daughter Elizabeth Peabody Kenny (Essex Institute, Salem)

Top: The Country Rocking Horse, illustration in St. Nicholas Magazine, 1870

Facing: Rocking horse with flynet, 24" high (American Museum in Britain)

Rocking-Horses & Go-Chairs.

WILLIAM LONG,

Cabinet-Maker and *Carver*, from *London*,
At his House in Union ſtreet, two Doors eaſt of Second
ſtreet,

RESPECTFULLY informs the Ladies and Gentle-men of this city, that he makes Rocking-Horſes in the neateſt and beſt manner, to teach children to ride and give them a wholeſome and pleaſing exerciſe: he makes Go-Chairs on the neweſt and beſt conſtuction, for the eaſe and comfort of thoſe, who by gout or rheumatic pains, are deprived of the uſe of their limbs, as they can move themſelves from room to room, on one floor, without the aſſiſtance of a ſervant, with eaſe and expedition; if they want to take the air in their garden, there it will be found uſeful—This chair has been highly approved of by the Royal Society in Lon-don, and by many of the firſt phyſicians in Europe.

Thoſe who want any of the above work, the ſubſcri-ber will wait on them at a ſhort notice. 3ſm d.

Advertisement in the Pennsylvania Packet of September 10th 1785

It is not until 1785 that we get the first indications that rocking horses were being made on a commercial basis. A cabinet maker and carver from London, William Long was making rocking horses. He staple lines seem to have been sofas and breakfast tables. In the Pennsylvania Packet on September 10th 1785 he 'respectfully informs the ladies and gentlemen of Philadelphia that he makes rocking horses in the neatest and best manner'. Some fifty years later we learn of another carver, Woodbury Gerrish of Portsmouth, New Hampshire who in addition to carving splendid ships' figureheads made rocking horses, furniture and coffins for his partner who was also the local undertaker.

From then on, during the course of the 19th century, we can witness the creation of some of the most original and beautiful horses by enterprising businessmen who added the making of horses to their many other commercial activities. In the following pages are notes on three of the most remarkable of these firms. Benjamin Potter Crandall and his son Jesse; Morton B. Converse and his son Atherton; and P. J. Marqua. There are also notes and illustrations of some of the other American manufacturers who made rocking horses between 1785 and 1930.

Shooflies and the Crandall Family

In 1941, Mr Peter Larsen carried out extensive research on two American rocking horses. Here are extracts from the data report sheets he made for the Index for American Design at the National Gallery of Art in Washington.

The first horse and the largest measured 21″ high, on rockers measuring 42″. It was found in

Williamsport, Pennsylvania. "The entire figure," says the report, "is painted yellow and the rockers red. Burnt with hot dies into the underface of the body is the inscription

B.P. Crandall:
47 Courtlandt St. N.Y.

The report continues "The body is carved from a single block of pine. The head and neck are carved from another single block. They are held together by glue reinforced by sheet iron plates applied with screws on both sides of the figure. The four separate flat legs are mortised into the underside of the body and secured with glue. The figure is mounted upon a pair of rockers and secured by iron screws applied through the lower end of the legs. Each of the rockers is made from separate front and back halves held together by iron nails driven into a transverse frame which is covered with an oblong platform. The front and back parts of the saddle are set and glued into transverse slots cut into the top face of the figure. The ears and the harness on the head and neck are of leather applied with iron tacks. The bit is made from round iron wire and the tail from horse hair."

The second horse measuring 16″ high was found in White Plains, New York. It had lost its rockers, it was painted orange and decorated with large black and red spots. It was stamped underneath with the same dies as the larger horse. Both horses were dated by Peter Larsen as having been made between 1853 and 1856. He adds that "Crandall is listed in New York street directories up to 1890 as a carpenter, a maker of wagons, carriages, perambulators, hobby horses and velocipedes." He gives several addresses for B.P. Crandall notably 49 Courtlandt Street and 469 Grand.

The complexities of the Crandall family network have been unravelled by Mrs Inez McClintock in her book 'Toys in America'. Suffice to say here that there are two main strands; that of Charles M. Crandall of Covington, Pennsylvania, inventor of innumerable games interlocking acrobats, circus animals, building blocks other wooden toys, and that of Benjamin Potter Crandall of New York and his four sons.

The Crandall family originally came from around Hopkinton, in Rhode Island. In 1845 Benjamin Potter Crandall moved to New York and first produced a kind of rocking chair called the Criket whose flat board sides bore some resemblance to a horse. He and his sons then produced a few stuffed horses made from real hides, then wooden horses on bow rockers, or on springs

Rocking horse made by Benjamin P. Crandall (Index of American Design, Washington) Watercolour by Mina Lowry

fixed to a platform, and finally at the turn of the century self-propelling horses which could buck and travel across the floor. These were known as Teddy Rough Riders.

Benjamin Potter's son Jesse is, however, best remembered for the rocking seat he patented in May 1859. This was perhaps inspired by a rocking cradle that was patented in February of the same year by Arad & Daniel Woodworth of Boston and which consisted of a head and neck of a horse combined with a hollow box or cradle. The Crandall toy patented three months later consisted of two boards in the shape of a horse with a seat between them. Jesse A. Crandall then baptised this new rocking toy a Shoofly and it enjoyed a huge success.

What is a Shoofly? American dictionaries give a bewildering number of definitions. *Random House Dictionary* tells us that it is a clover broom, a finger-like mechanism used by printers, a temporary track on the railroad. *The American Dialect Dictionary*

states however that it is a large bow tie, a large low vehicle with two rows of seats lengthwise, a kind of hobby horse. Harold Wentworth's confuses the issue further by stating that a shoo-fly is a mild expression of surprise, or a plain clothes police officer or a traverse track in a mine. While Webster declares firmly, a shoofly is a kind of shuffling dance or a civil war nonsense song called 'Shoofly don't bother me' perhaps an early version of a 1948 pop song "Shoofly Pie and Apple Pie Dowdy".

All authorities agree that a shoofly pie is made from sweet crumb, brown sugar and molasses just like an English treacle tart and that it attracted flies that had to be shooed away.

There is also a minor question of spelling. The 1914 catalogue of Butler Bros. has a heading 'Shooflys' whereas the Sears Roebuck catalogue for the same date proclaims 'Shooflies'. No one seems quite sure whether the word should be hyphened or not.

Rocking horse, Benjamin P. Crandall, 1853-1856 (Index of American Design, Washington)

Right: Advertisement in Playthings 1907 for 'The Teddy Horse or Rough Rider horse that bucks and travels' which could also be used as a conventional rocking horse. Patent by Jesse Crandall at the end of the 19th century

Facing: A Crandall type rocking horse (The Abby Aldrich Rockefeller Collection, Williamsbury)

70

Morton E. Converse & Son and the Whitney Reed Chair Co.

Morton E. Converse was born in Rindge, New Hampshire. As a young man he spent three years fighting in the Civil War. In 1878 he went to Winchenton, Massachusetts and set up a small factory making inexpensive punnets for strawberries and other fruits. Quite by accident he entered the toy business. His youngest daughter was ill in bed and to amuse her he whittled some little wooden dishes, and by adding legs to a wooden collar box, made a table to put them on. The result was so attractive that he sold the idea to two collar manufacturers in New York. He moved on to manufacturing wooden puzzles, Noah's Arks and then rocking horses which became the symbol of his ever growing business.

Morton E. Converse had a genius for finding manufacturing short cuts. For his horses he devised

Mr. Morton E. Converse (Winchenton Historical Society)
Above: Morton E. Converse factory at Winchenton

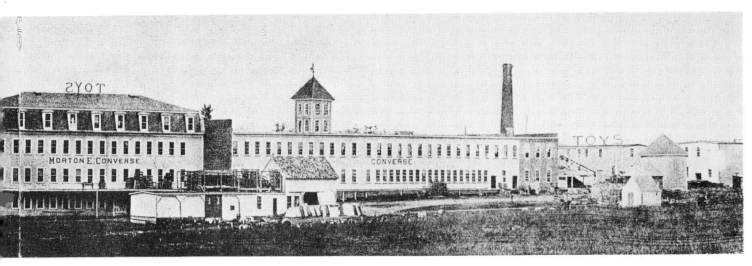

a copying block with knives that followed a master model, and which shaped other blocks of wood automatically. Only the final finishes on the head were done by hand. The horses were dipped and spray painted. The larger, more expensive horses were, however, covered with real hide. By 1890 the firm was making 15,000 rocking horses a year, the factories covered six acres and Winchenton was known as Toy Town – The Nuremberg of America.

To celebrate the one hundred and fiftieth centenary of the town Morton E. Converse had a huge 14′, horse built. For many years afterwards it stood in the square near the railway station, next to the Toy Town Tavern. The horse has now succumbed to old age and is stored away, waiting hopefully for sufficient funds to be collected locally either to restore him to his former self or create a replica.

Morton E. Converse's son entered his father's business in 1890. He became one of the founder

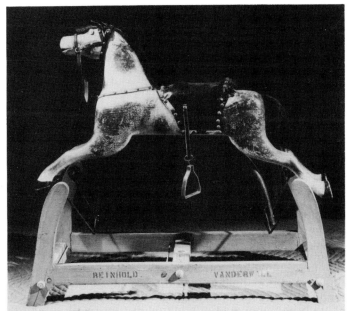

Converse type rocking horse 1890, 24″ high, painted dark brown on red rockers (Museums at Stony Brook, New York)

members of the Toy Manufacturers of the USA and ran the family business until its decline in 1930.

The Converse rocking horses were mounted on a characteristic swinging device – similar to that used by Lines Bros. in their Jubilee rocker of 1911. In the 1912 Sears Roebuck catalogue four sizes and prices of Converse horses are advertised.

Twenty-five miles away from Winchenton at Leominster another firm, The Whitney Reed Chair Co. was also making rocking horses. A letter

Advertisement in Playthings 1906 for Morton E. Converse horse

Facing: Shoofly late 19th century and detail of the painted platform (Essex Institute, Salem)

written on February 2nd 1928 by the Converse firm to Mr Green proposes some kind of merger.

'The horse business has dropped off considerably during the past several years. There is hardly enough business to keep either of us going on this line. Really either Whitney Reed or ourselves should make all of the horses, one purchases from the other. We are perfectly willing that you should make all our horses.'

Two years later the firm of Morton E. Converse had closed down.

In 1952 the Boston firm of M. Sharf & Co. was still advertising Whitney Reed horses: on bow rockers (No. 138) on safety stands (No. 65) and three sizes of Converse type of swing horses.

How then to distinguish a Morton E. Converse original from a Whitney Reed horse? Mrs Lois Greenwood, Curator of The Winchendon Historical Society says that a member of the Converse family told her "that the only way you could tell a Converse horse from any other type, such as a Whitney Reed; was that the bow was one piece of flat bentwood". Mrs Greenwood mentions seeing a Whitney Reed horse which had a bow made of two parallel dowels "in place of the flat one piece of wood".

Somewhere too there may be a Converse horse which can waggle its ears as in October 1896 Morton E. Converse took out letters patent concerning an invention; a rocking horse with movable ears "whereby the pleasure derived from moving the same will add to the amusement value of the horse. This movement of the ears is intended to make the horse more lifelike, such for instance, as the appearance of getting ready to bite."

Painted Platforms

"Rosebud" murmurs Citizen Kane on his deathbed, as the glass snowstorm slips from his fingers. The enigma of this strange last word is revealed in the final shot of this memorable film, as an old wooden sleigh is thrown on a bonfire, the flames light up for the last time, a naive bunch of roses painted on its base, the dead magnate's last link with his humble early childhood and his mother from whom he was so cruelly parted.

Could this painted sleigh have come from the same stable as the horses whose footrests are decorated with similar simple folk paintings? A

horse in the Museum at Stony Brook has roses painted on the platform between the rockers, a stylised tulip adorns the platform of a horse in the Philadelphia Museum of Art. Shooflies in the Essex Institute at Salem have flowers on their sides. A beautiful sailing ship floats somewhat incongruously on the base of a rocking horse owned by Mr Bernard Barenholtz. An oval painting of a landscape can be discerned on a horse mounted on black painted rockers outlined with yellow curlicues which is now in the Margaret Woodbury Strong Museum. Another small horse in the DAR Museum in Washington has a now rather battered horse and rider galloping away on its footrest.

These charming "platform pictures" seem to be a characteristic of American rocking horses, and as they bear a certain family likeness to those branded with Benjamin Potter Crandall's name, they have been grouped together in the following pages.

Horse in Bernard Barenholtz's collection with painted ship on platform

Top: Crandall type wooden horse with tulip design on platform (Philadelphia Museum of Art)

Top right: Crandall type rocking horse with rose design on platform (Museums at Stony Brook)

Facing: Details of painted platforms. Watercolours by Maria Wood

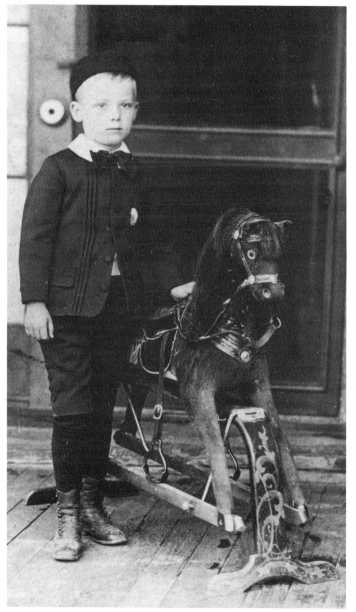

P.J. Marqua and Safety Rockers

The firm of P.J. Marqua was established in Cincinnati, Ohio in 1856. They were manufacturers of basketware, childrens carriages and cabs. The firm is best known, however for the two patents which it took out for new types of rocking horses. The first which dates from 1865 was for a rearing rocking horse on which two or more children could ride at the same time. The illustration in the pages devoted to American patents shows how the inequalities in the weights of the children riding this horse was compensated by an ingenious method of counter balancing and the use of a special form of spring. The second patent dated October 1878 was the more revolutionary, by mounting the horses on safety stands which allowed the child to rock to and fro instead of up and down was soon adapted and copied by many other manufacturers.

In the New Hampshire Historical Society collection there is a splendid horse called Tony who belonged to Phineas Frank Russell Jnr. (1880 – 1950) of East Hebron.

Stencilled on the red base is Marqua, Hobby – Patented October 1878. Shortly after this date the firm changed its name to Bently & Marqua and then in 1910 to Marqua & Skinner Carriage and Toy Co. It was situated on Fourth and Main Street, Cincinnati.

Left: Marqua type skin covered rocking horse called Ulysses with its first owner Robert Cortes Holliday (The Children's Museum, Indianapolis)

Facing: 'Tony', belonged to Phineas Frank Russell Jnr. (1880-1950) of East Hebron, New Hampshire. Tony is dapplegrey with leather saddle and bridle and horsehair mane and tail. Stencilled on the base is Marqua, Hobby/Patented Oct. 1878' (New Hampshire Historical Society)

American Rocking Horses 1785–1989

1785-1933 LONG, William,
Union Street, Philadelphia, Pennsylvania.
Rocking horses and go-chairs. In July 1788 William Long had moved to Fourth Street and was advertising French sofas, chairs and new fashioned cadet breakfast tables. In 1796 the Philadelphia Directory lists him at Chestnut Street and two years later at the corner of Seventh and Chestnut Street. By 1807 he had moved to Juniper Lane. It is possible that his horses were sold in the toy shop run by John and William Wigglesworth.

1840-1870 CRANDALL, Benjamin Potter,
Westerley, Rhode Island, & 49 Courtlandt Street, New York.
Rocking horses and velocipedes. Succeeded by his sons, Charles T. Crandall and Jesse A. Crandall of New York. *See previous pages*

1840 GERRISH, Woodbury C.
14/16 Daniel Street, Portsmouth, New Hampshire.
Carver of ships' figureheads. Notably that of Benjamin Franklin which adorned the US Ship of the Line Franklin in 1853 and of a splendid Goddess of Victory now in the Portsmouth Yacht Club. In the 1875 Portsmouth Directory Woodbury Gerrish is listed together with Josiah F. Adams as coffin manufacturers, undertakers and ships' carvers, at 14 & 16 Daniel Street, Portsmouth. Woodbury Gerrish also made rocking horses. In earlier directories he is listed as a cabinet maker and an ornamental carver and it is thought that one of his rocking horses is in the Henry Ford Museum, Dearborn, Michigan.

1843 COX, Gideon
335 & 337 High Street, Philadelphia, Pennsylvania.
McCleary's Philadelphia Directory of 1843 lists Gideon Cox as running a dry goods, wooden and variety store. He is also listed as supplying rocking horses.

1847-1857 BUSHELLI, E.W.
Philadelphia, Pennsylvania.
Rocking horses & velocipedes. After 1857 they became Bushnell & Tull.

1849-50 HENDERSON, E. & CO.
New Hartford, Connecticut.
Rocking horses.

1850-1868 CHRISTIAN, A. & SON.
New York.
Manufactured horses of various kinds including velocipedes, rocking horses and various carriages. Sometimes known as Christian & Son, after 1868 as Christian & Dare. In 1880 taken over by Hoffmere Kelsey & Cornwall.

1851 CRANDALL & McKINSTRY
469 Grand, New York.
Rocking horses.

1856 BROWN & EGGLESTON
New York.
Rocking horses and propellers.

1856 KINGHAM
82 Lincoln Street,
Boston, Massachusetts.
Rocking horses & propellers. After 1855 Snow & Kingman.

Leaping horse by Marqua from Inez McClintock's 'Toys in America'

1856 MARQUA, P.J.
4th & Main Street,
Cincinnati, Ohio.
See previous pages.

1857 BUSHELL & TULL
Philadelphia, Pennsylvania.
Rocking horses & velocipedes.

1859 HITCHCOCK, M.T.
76 Sudbury Street,
Boston, Massachusetts.
Patented horse-head rocking chair with
Arad & Daniel Woodworth. Patent No.
23003. (U.S. Patent Office) These rocking
horse cradles sold by Isaac B. Rich at 76
Sudbury Street, Boston, 1860-1862. Arad
Woodworth listed in Boston City
Directories from 1853 as a machinist.

1859 WOODWORTH, Arad & Daniel
Patented horse-head chair with M.J.
Hitchcock.

1860 ASKAM & Son
Philadelphia, Pennsylvania.
Rocking horses and propellers.

1860 TIBBALS, Lewis P.
510 Broadway,
Opp. St. Nicholas Hotel, New York.
Spring and cantering horses.

Spring Rocking-Horses.
Cantering Horses.
Baby-Tenders.
Patent Swings.
Children's Carriages.
Drums, Sleds, and Toys.
LEWIS TIBBALS,
510 Broadway,
Opposite St. Nicholas Hotel.
N B —Invalid Chairs and
Propellers on hand and made
to order.

1860 WHITNEY, F.A.
Leominster, Massachusetts.
Rocking horses. See Whitney Reed Chair
Co. 1863

CHRISTMAS GIFTS.
Hobby Horses, Velocipides,
Sleighs, Carts, Wagons, Sleds,
&c., Wholesale and Retail, by
the Manufacturer,
J. A. YOST,
214 DOCK Street, and THIRD Street, and GIRARD
Avenue.   4p2-11-2m

1860-1890 YOST, J.A.
214 Dock Street & Third Street &
Girard Avenue,
Philadelphia, Pennsylvania.
Rocking horses & velocipedes.

1864 MEINECKE, A & Son
Milwaukee, Wisconsin.
Rocking horses and shooflies with silver
plated brand mark. Adolf Meinecke was
born in 1830 near Bremmen in Germany.
He came to America in 1848 and was
employed by an importing firm in New
York. In 1853 he settled in Milwaukee
selling imported German toys and some
made in the USA. In 1864 Adolf
Meinecke started the manufacture of
Willow baskets that were the basis of the
firm's fortunes. The Milwaukee Willow
Works by 1870 occupied a large block on
Mason Street and employed over three
hundred workers making baskets
children's carriages rattan cradles and
chairs and other items of furniture. They
also made wooden clogs, croquet sets, toy
wagons and rocking horses which carried
a silver plated brand mark. The firm of
Adolf Meinecke & Son is listed in the
Milwaukee City Directory until 1929.

A. MEINECKE & SON,
— MANUFACTURERS OF —
BAMBOO AND PUNJAB FURNITURE NOVELTIES.
Easels, Screens, Tables, Chairs, Stools, Bunk Shelves, Brackets, Standing
Cabinets, Whatnots, Umbrella Stands, Pedestals, Etc.

CHILDREN'S CARRIAGES.
Beautiful Styles, Latest Novelties in Bodies, such as Bamboo
Rod, Oak Framed, Etc.

MILWAUKEE, WIS.

SMITH WOOD

1865-1912 SMITH WOOD PRODUCTS
Brattleboro, Vermont.

The firm of S.A. Smith started by making baby carriages. In 1889 the firm changed its name to S.A. Smith & Co. and started to manufacture children's toys. The S.A. Smith line included Shooflies, rocking horses, and hobby horses.

1865 VANDERBILT & McQUEEN
New York.

Rocking horses.

1866-1870 BROWN, J.H.
449 West Street, New York.

Patented on December 11th, 1866 a spring horse. Could be connected with Thomas Brown and Elder & Brown who between 1867 and 1870 are listed as dealing with rocking horses.

1867-1890 BOYLSTON, S. & F.
New York, & Rowayton, Connecticut.

Rocking horses.

1867 DARE, C.W.F
New York

See A. Christian.

1867-1870 FISHER, George
New York.

Rocking horses.

1867 METZLER & COWPERTHWAITE
New York.

Rocking horses.

1867 WASHBURN, Daniel T.
New York

Rocking horses.

1868-1880 CHRISTIAN DARE
New York.

Rocking horses, propellers and velocipedes.

1868-1870 STEWART & CORBETT
New York.

Spring & rocking horses, propellers.

1868 WENTWORTH, J
Boston, Massachusetts.

Rocking horses.

1869-1911 MACE, L.H. & CO.
East Houston Street, New York.

Advertised rocking horses.

Advertisement in Playthings 1911. Horse sold by L. H. Mace & Co. Manufacturers of Mace refrigerators who also advertised skin, plush covered, swinging, rocking platform combination horse

1871 KIRSCH, Ernst
Pleasant Street, nr. Post Office, Amesbury, Massachusetts.

Was a carriage bodymaker who worked for the carriage manufacturers Patten and Blaisdell whose factory was on Pleasant Street. His name appears only once in the Amesbury Directory 1872 the year after he had taken out a patent for a bentwood rocking horse which is one of the most beautiful and original of all the rocking horses made in America. It would seem that he made these horses privately and not for the firm he worked for.

1873 QUIGG, J.F.
Chicago, Illinois.

Rocking horses.

1873-1952 WHITNEY REED CHAIR CO.
Leominster, Massachusetts.

The predecessors of this firm were established in 1860 in Leominster, Mass. and were known successively as F.A. Whitney and W.A. Reed Toy Co. According to the local newspaper the *Leominster Enterprise* in its Souvenir Edition of 1873-1897 the Whitney Reed Chair Co. was one of the largest and best appointed businesses in Leominster. The firm made dolls' carriages, childrens' chairs, galloping and rocking horses as well as shooflies. The firm is said to have produced 40,000 rocking horses annually and employed 250 people. In 1952 the Whitney Reed horses were still featured in the catalogue of M. Sharf & Co., Boston; they listed three sizes of swinging horses, a moulded rocking horse on 30" bow

WHITNEY REED

rockers, a simplified rocking horse for 1 to 6 year olds, a bouncing contraption called 'Cal's Colt' and a horse tricycle called 'Battle Wagon'. The Whitney Reed Chair Co. was only 25 miles from the Converse factory at Winchenton. In February 1928 Mr A. Converse wrote to Mr Green of the Whitney Reed Chair Co. suggesting some kind of merger concerning the manufacturer of rocking horses but two years later the Converse factory had closed down.

1875 KIP MANUFACTURING CO.
Keene, New York.
Rocking horses.

1878 BENTLEY & MARQUA
Cincinnati, Ohio.
Successors to Marqua, P.A.

1878 CONVERSE, Morton E.
Winchendon, Massachusetts.
See previous pages.

1878-1883 MASON & CONVERSE
Winchendon, Massachusetts.
See previous pages.

1878 PEABODY & WHITNEY
Boston, Massachusetts.
See Whitney Reed Chair Co.

1880-1890 TRAVERS, George W.
New York
Rocking horses, velocipedes.

1883 MECKY, A.
Philadelphia, Pennsylvania.
Rocking horses & propellers.

1890-1930 CONVERSE, Atherton D.
See previous pages

1904 NATIONAL NOVELTY CO.
826-828 Broadway, New York.
A combination platform and rocking horse, possibly imported. Firm taken over by Nicholas N. Colwell in 1908.

1906 HALL CAR MANUFACTURING CO.
Northville, Michigan.
Shooflies – Agents Strobel & Wilkin, New York.

1907 STEINFELD BROS.
620 Broadway, New York.
Sold shooflies.

TECUMSEH

1907 TECUMSEH MANUFACTURING CO.
Tecumseh, Michigan.
Embossed shoofly rockers Agents: Strobel & Wilkin Co., Baker & Bigler, In 1897 listed in local directory as Tecumseh Manufacturing Co. Manufacturers of sash windows, doors and blinds. Later directories listed as Tecumseh Sash & Door Co., Pearle Street, Tecumseh, Michigan.

1908 COLWELL, Nicolas H.
See National Novelty Co.

1909-1915 ARNEY SPECIALITY CO.
State Street, Port Huron, Michigan.
Made wooden horses with pedals and reins attached to carts which could carry one or two children. They also made special furniture, amusement devices and "auto ponies". In 1912 the firm moved to Water Street.

1909 INTER-STATE MANUFACTURING CO.
Port Huron, Michigan.
Rocking horses.

1910   HARDWARE &
WOODENWARE
MANUFACTURING CO.
603–697 Broadway, New York.
Fred W. Crandall. Rocking chair with
horses head. Also agents for Whitney
Reed Chair Co. and S.A. Smith horses.

1911   GIBBS TOYS,
Canton, Ohio.
Small 9″ rocking horses.

1912   BENNER
MANUFACTURING CO.
Lancaster, Pennsylvania.
Shooflies, Company was founded by
Joseph T. Brennman and John H.
Hartman when they took over the assets
of the Hubley Manufacturing Co.
founded in 1894 and who made a variety
of wooden toys.

BENNER LINE

1919–1941   JANESVILLE
PRODUCTS CO.
Dept 120, Janesville, Wisconsin.
Janesville has been identified with the
manufacture and assembly of practically
anything that rolled on wheels. The first
carriage and wagon factory was started in
1848. The Janesville Products Co. began
in 1885 but was known as The Lawrence

Most THRILLING
ACTION
of ALL SPRING
Riding Toys
the
ROLY RIDERS

Carriage Works then the Wisconsin
Carriage Co. In 1910 the firm branched
out into the manufacture of The Wisco
Automobile but this early car was not
successful and they reverted to the buggy
business. In the 1930's during the years of
depression the Company ventured into
the toy market manufacturing a baseball
game and some simple rocking horses
called 'Roly Riders', a simplified rocking
seat called the 'Bucky Horse'. The same
spring mechanism was applied to their
'Jacky Rabbit', 'Go Goosey' and 'Wingy
Plane' models. The firm also
manufactured other childrens' vehicles
and full-scale furniture until 1941 when
the factory closed down.

1926   MENGEL PLAYTHINGS INC.
Louisville, Kentucky.
Made 'Rock-a-Tot', a rocking chair like a
cockerel.

1930   ANIMAL
MANUFACTURING CO.
Carbondale, Illinois.
'The Beauty Pony', a horse on wheels.

1930   GOLDSTEIN, Charles & Victor
Jones Street, New York.
'Rambling Rob' and 'Bucking Bob'
horses.

GOLDSTEIN

1931–1933   COROZAN
MANUFACTURING CO.
Section Avenue & Foraker Avenue
Norwood, Cincinatti, Ohio.
Manufacturers of sheet metal parts,
automobile radiators, tool boxes and
bathroom cabinets. In 1931 they
advertised in *Playthings* the 'Nobby
Hobby Horse.'

Velocipedes 1860-1912

1850 STEELE, H.B.
Winchester, Connecticut.

Dr Harvey B. Steele was a leading doctor in Hartford, Connecticut. A Democratic politician who became a member of the General Assembly in 1872 and of the Senate in 1874. At the same time he carried out the functions of Postmaster of West Winsted. In addition to all these duties he set up a factory making cab wheels, wagons, carriages and velocipedes. This was burnt down in 1857 but Dr Steele immediately started up another factory the Eagle Scythe Works employing sixteen men and forty women.

1857 COLBY BROS.
Waterbury, Vermont.

The first products of this firm were made of willow. Dolls' carriages and baskets. In 1860 George Colby invented a new type of clothes wringer which became the foundation of the firm's fortunes. They continued, however, to make wooden toys, notable boats and velocipedes.

1875 FRALEY, G.W.
Philadelphia, Pennsylvania.
Velocipedes.

1875 PICKERING, Thomas
Portland, Connecticut.
Velocipedes.

1879 BARNES & CO.
Covington, Kentucky.
Velocipedes.

1880 TRICYCLE MANUFACTURING CO.
Springfield, Ohio.

Manufacturers of children's carriages boys wagons, velocipedes and dolls carriages. The speciality of this firm were steel wheels suitable for all kinds of vehicles.

1886-1887 YAGGY & KINLEY
Chicago, Illinois.
Velocipedes, The firm was also known as Western Toy Co.

CENTRAL

1912 CENTRAL WHEEL & MANUFACTURING CO.
Sturgis, Michigan.

'Bucking Bronco'. A horse tricycle which gave the movement of a galloping horse, the large horses were also sold with an attachment for the front axle which enabled a small child to ride it safely.

Present Day Makers 1988

CHERMAC INTERNATIONAL
1869 Graig Park Court, St. Louis,
Missouri 63146.

Handpainted rocking horse moulded in
high-density polyurethane with high
gloss non-toxic finish. Mounted on a
tubular steel brass painted base. This
'Carousel Joy Rocker' was originally
designed in 1948 by Mr Morris Haas and
was carved in wood. Chermac also
produce the 'Joy Rider Carousel' – 30"
high and 4' in diameter consisting of three
horses on a merry-go-round base. This
too was originally designed by Mr Morris
Hass.

CHERRY TREE TOYS

CHERRY TREE TOYS INC.
P.O. Box 369, 408 S. Jefferson,
Belmont, Ohio 43718.

The original toys of this Ohio firm were
all made of cherry wood. Today they are
one of America's leading suppliers of parts
and accessories for making toys,
whirligigs, crafts and furniture. They
produce a simple wooden horse on bow
rockers.

MAPES INDUSTRIES INC.
6 Grace Avenue, Great Neck,
New York 11021

Manufacturers of the 'Pony-Pet' rocking
horse in three different sizes on bow
rockers. Walnut finished wood covered in
a high pile carpet material.

VENTURE RIDE MFG. INC.
Route 8, Box 11 C, Highway 14,
Greer, South Carolina 29651.

One of the largest manufacturers of
children's rides in the United States. In
1984 the President, Mr Jerry L. Barber
took a horse from the firm's merry-go-
round, made a rocker base for it for his
young daughter to use in the nursery.
Since then they have started to market a
similar horse for private customers. The
horses made by Venture Manufacturing
were designed by Lois Shaffer and
moulded in resin. They are very popular
as replacement horses on traditional
merry-go-rounds as the owners have sold
their wooden horses to collectors.

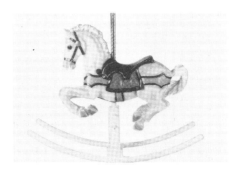

VENTURE RIDE

WELSH & Co.
1535 South 8th Street, St. Louis,
Missouri 63104.

Manufacturers of three sizes of rocking
horses on bow rockers in oak or walnut
finishes with either wool or rope manes.
They also make 'Woody' – a horse on
wheels, and 'Prancer' – a stick hobby horse
both in natural finish with rope manes.

WELSH

Repairs to Old Horses

In the course of the research for this book I
have been given the names of people who
have restored the horses on display in
several Museums but only one has wished
us to give his name. He is Mr Tony
Orlando of 6661 Norborn, Dearborn
Hgts, Michigan 48127. (Tel: (313) 561-
5072). For the past 15 years he has dealt
with the conservation and restoration of
antique carousel figures and rocking horses.

SWINGING HOBBY HORSES.

One of the highest grade made, real skin covered with long mane and tail, beautifully formed body, genuine leather bridle with metal bit, handsome genuine leather removable saddle with very fancy decorated blanket having heavy gilt fringe. Horseshoes and stirrups of metal gilded, the stirrup straps being adjustable in length to 15 inches from saddle. Glass eyes, lifelike appearance. Height, over all, 33 inches; from hoof to hoof, 38½ inches. Shipping weight, 40 lbs.
No. 49K3066¼ Price...... **$10.50**

Nice dapple gray finish swinging hobby horse. Height of saddle from floor, 24½ inches; length of horse over all, 36½ inches; height over all, 32 inches. Stirrups adjustable to 12½ inches from saddle. Each carefully packed in crate for shipment.
Shipping weight, 25 pounds.
No. 49K3033¼ Price........ **$6.85**

Swinging Horse, $2.25.

Enameled air brush finish, 42 inches long, 29 inches to top of head. Nicely red enameled and striped stand. English saddle in enamel cloth, enamel cloth saddle flaps trimmed with fancy colored fringe, has hair mane and tail, stirrups, martingales with rings, heavy breast band. Shipping weight, about 22 pounds.
No. 49K3078¼ Price........ **$2.25**

Large Size Hobby Horse. Graceful figure, perfect shape, hand carved legs and hoofs. White enameled dapple gray color, real metal horseshoes, long heavy mane and tail, glass eyes, leather bridle, metal gag bit, martingale, leather reins, heavily padded leather saddle with plush saddle skirt and gilt stirrups, and large fancy plush blanket with gilt fringe. Improved swinging attachment. Height of saddle from floor, 26½ in; length bottom stirrup from top saddle adjustable to 15 in; length of horse over all, 40½ in.; height of horse from floor, 35½ in. Shipping wt., 30 lbs.
No. 49K3032¼ Price........ **$8.95**

Nice dapple gray finish swinging hobby horse, but with cheaper trimmings than above. Has flowing mane and tail, heavily padded saddle, stirrups, painted eyes, leather reins and same easy swinging attachment. Height of saddle from floor, 24½ inches. Stirrups adjustable to 13½ inches from saddle.
Shipping weight, 20 pounds.
No. 49K3034¼ Price........ **$4.65**
Similar to the above, but smaller. Height of saddle from floor, 23½ in.; stirrups adjustable to 13½ in. from saddle; length of horse over all, 34½ in.; ht. over all, 29½ in. Ship. wt., 20 lbs.
No. 49K3035¼ Price........ **$3.68**

Solid oak, nicely stained in natural colors; hair mane, leather reins, imitation eyes. Just the thing for a young child. Height, 9 inches from floor; length, 15 inches. Regular $1.50 value. Shipping wt., 10 lbs.
No. 49K3031¼ Price..... **98c**

Beautifully painted in natural colors. Has swinging toy box, seat and back, fancy reed effect basket. Very strongly made. Has fancy plush cushion and back pad, imitation painted harness and mane. Good value. Size, 35x23½ inches. Shipping weight, 20 lbs.
No. 49K3041¼ Price........ **$2.79**

$2.79

Head of wood in natural colors, imitation leather harness, reins and ears, real hair mane, reed basket seat. Nicely painted and decorated. Size, 43 x 24 inches. Shipping weight, 15 pounds.
No. 49K3077¼ Price........ **$2.95**

Size, 21 x 38 inches. The body is made of very fancy reed, best quality, strong and durable. Seat upholstered in fine velour, with back cushions of the same material. Shipping weight, carefully crated, 15 pounds.
No. 49K3065¼ Price........ **$2.25**

Swinging Shoo-Fly Rocking Horse.
Size, 24 x 32 inches. Beautifully painted, has toy box, seat and back upholstered in cretonne, horses suspended on swinging frame. Not easy to tip over. Shipping wt., 15 lbs.

No. 49K3038¼ Price........ **$1.89**

From Sears, Roebuck & Co catalogue 1912

87

American Patents

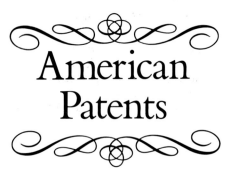

1859 WOODWORTH, Arad & Daniel & HITCHCOCK, M.T.
Boston, County of Suffolk, Massachusetts.

Head and neck of a horse combined with a hollow box or cradle which rocks longitudinally.
US Patent No. 23.003 February 15th 1859.

1859 CRANDALL, Jesse A.
(Son of Benjamin Potter Crandall)
New York

Improvements to the box on rockers by means of flat wound springs, elastic and thumbs screws to give an easy rocking motion without the jar of rockers on the floor and wear and tear of carpet.
US Patent No. 24.008 May 17th 1859.

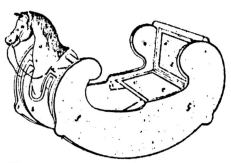

1861 CRANDALL, Jesse A.
New York,

Spring rocking horse or a box or seat attached to a strong spring.
US Patent No. 31.571 February 26th 1861.

1861 CHRISTIAN, Andrew
New York.

A more secure method of mounting the rocking horse onto the platform by means of springs attached between the two front legs of the horse.
US Patent No. 31,869 April 2nd 1862.

1862 CRANDALL, Jesse A.
New York.

Another variation on the spring rocking horse.
US Patent 1.287 March 11th 1862.

1865 MARQUA, P.J.
Cincinnati, Ohio.

Rearing rocking horse and seat which works by means of an India rubber thong and a flexible beam fixed to the underside of the horse.
US Patent 16.258 February 7th 1865.

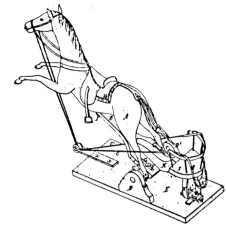

1866   THORPE, T. P.
New York.

A complicated exercising machine. The child was supposed to put its legs through the holes O O – a dangerous looking machine.
US Patent No. 53,900 April 10th 1866.

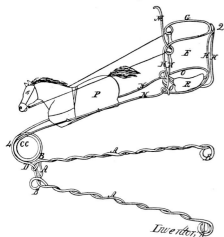

1866   BROWN, John H.
449 West Street, New York.

A spring rocking horse operated by means of a spiral or tension spring.
US Patent 60.336 December 11th 1866.

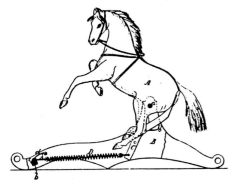

1868   RICH, Charles
Poughkeepsie, New York.

A baby jumper activated by a complicated spring mechanism.
US Patent No. 82,992 October 13th 1868.

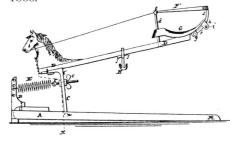

1869   BERG, William & STEPHAN, Mathias
Canton, Stark, Ohio.

An improved baby jumper.
US Patent No. 90,985 June 8th 1869.

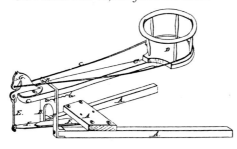

1870   CRANDALL, Benjamin Potter
New York.

A rocking horse mounted on a flat bed and having its seat out of centre, in combination with spring-strips secured to the rockers and the bed.
US Patent No. 98,929 January 18th 1870.

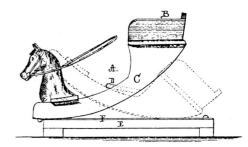

1871   KIRSCH, Ernst.
South Amesbury, Massachusetts.
Light and springy horse made from bent wood.
US Patent 121.945 December 19th 1871.

1878   MARQUA, P.J.
Cincinnati, Ohio.
Rocking horse on safety type swing rockers.
October 1878

1881   GOODSPEED, Albert.
Hubbardston, Massachusetts.
Spring horse on an 'X' shaped pedestal.
US Patent 244.586 July 19th 1881.

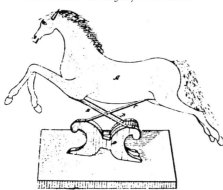

1882   SMALL, Herbert M.
Baldwinsville, Massachusetts.
'Rockermotive', a wheeled truck with horses's head on which is mounted a rocking seat.
US Patent 253.557 February 14th 1882.

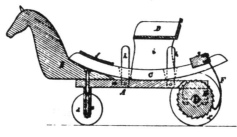

1882   SHEPARDSON, Cornelius
Casenovia, New York.
A rocking seat mounted on wheels which could be folded back when not in use.
US Patent 256.390 April 11th 1882.

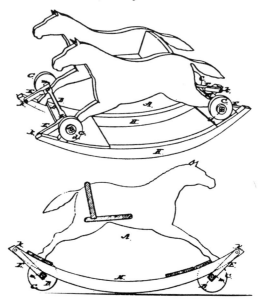

1882   CRANDALL, Jesse A.
New York.
Rocking horse and cradle. A variation on the shoofly with a seat fixed inside the toybox. The seat having a hinged back and foot rest which could be folded back to form a cradle.
US Patent 267.678 November 21st 1882

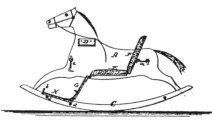

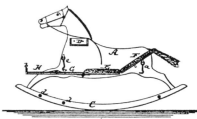

1883   CRANDALL, William Edwin
(brother of Jesse A.)
New York.
Rocking horse and gig. One or more horses plus a gig mounted on rockers.
US Patent 270.023 January 2nd 1883.

Ernst Kirsch, 1871 (Margaret Woodbury Strong Museum)

1883 CRANDALL, Jesse A.
New York.
Horse and carriage which gives the impression of movement whilst remaining stationary.
US Patent 270.891 January 23rd 1883.

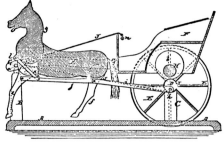

1889 CRANDALL, Jesse A.
New York.
'Babyjumper' rocking horse and seat which is set in motion by pulling on the reins.
US Patent 411.643 September 24th 1889.

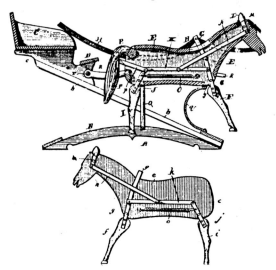

1890 BESSETTE, Frank B.
St. Cloud, Minnesota.
An all purpose horse which can be in turn a wheeled horse, a rocking horse, a cradle, a wagon, a stool and a table.
US Patent 419.405 January 19th 1890.

FIG.2.

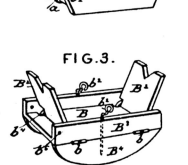

FIG.1.

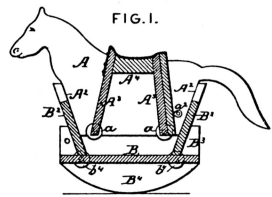

FIG.3.

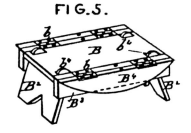

FIG. 4.

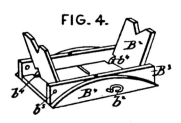

FIG.5.

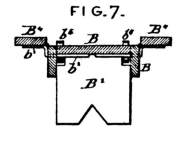

FIG.6.

FIG.7.

1890   WADE, George W.
Cadillac, Michigan.
Galloping rocking horse with auxiliary back legs fixed to a short set of extra rockers.
US Patent 420.844 February 4th 1890

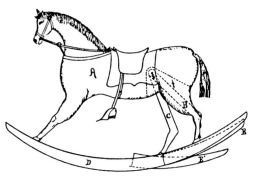

1896   CONVERSE, Morton E.
Winchendon, Massachusetts.
Rocking horse with moveable ears.
US Patent 570.002 October 27th 1896.

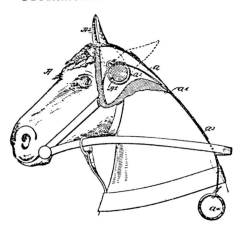

1899   WILFERT, Frank.
Leominster, Massachusetts.
Self-propelling rocking horse.
US Patent 618.155 January 24th 1899.

1926   SEDLACEK, John E.
Schuyler, Colfax, Nebraska.
A kind of combination of rocking seat and scooter.
US Patent No. 1,576,851 March 16th 1926.

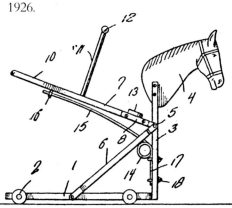

1927   SHERROD, William
Los Angeles, California.
A spring type rocking horse which could be adjusted according to children's weight and size.
US Patent No. 1,624,986 April 19th 1927.

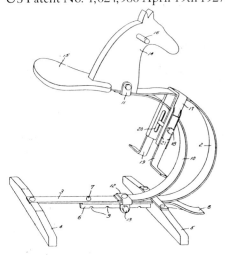

1928   CATTERLIN, Francis J.
Chicago, Illinois.
A contraption which he calls 'hobbyhorse and the like'.
US Patent No. 1,668,190 May 1st 1928.

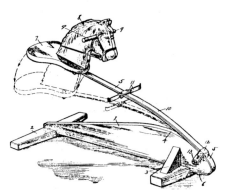

Pull-along horse (Victoria and Albert Museum)

Tricycle horse (Horniman Museum)

Old Horses At Rest

A number of stately homes and museums have old rocking horses on display. A 'Shire' publication, *'Discovering Toys and Toy Museums'*, by Pauline Flick, gives a useful list. Here are a few more, at home and abroad:

Great Britain
American Museum in Britain, Claverton Manor, Bath.
Aston Hall, Birmingham.
Cambo House, Cambo, Morpeth, Northumberland.
Cushing's Steam Museum, Thursford, Norfolk.
Hove Museum & Art Gallery, Hove, Sussex.
Laycock Abbey, Wiltshire.
London Museum, Barbican, London.
Lynn Museum, King's Lynn, Norfolk.
Madam Tussaud's at Wookey Hole Caves & Mill, nr. Wells, Somerset.
Museum of Childhood, Edinburgh, Scotland.
Museum of Childhood, Menai Bridge, Anglesey, North Wales.
Penrhyn Castle, Bangor, Gwynedd, North Wales.
Pollock's Toy Museum, 1 Scala Street, London W1.

Overseas
Bucks County Historical Society Museum, Doylestown, USA.
Ghent Folk Museum, Belgium.
Museum of the City of New York, 5th Avenue, New York, USA.
Patricia Mullins Collection, 83 St. David's St. Fitzroy, Melbourne, Australia.
Musèe Alsacien de Strasbourg, France.
Nordiska Museum, Stockholm, Sweden.

Europe

Ghent Folk Museum, Belgium.
Musee Alsacien de Strasbourg, France.
Nordiska Museum, Stockholm, Sweden.

America

Abby Aldrich Rockefeller Folk Art Center, Colonial
Williamsburg, Virginia.
Bucks County Historical Society Museum, Doylestown,
Pennsylvania.
Chicago Historical Society, Chicago, Illinois.
Childrens' Museum, Indianapolis, Indiana.
DAR Museum, Washington, District of Columbia.
Essex Institute, Salem, Massachusetts.
Henry Ford Museum, Deerborn, Michigan.
Margaret Woodbury Strong Museum, Rochester, New York.
Museum of the City of New York, New York.
New York Historical Society, New York.
New Hampshire Historical Society, Concord, New Hampshire.
Pennsylvania State Farm Museum, Landis Valley, Lancaster,
Pennsylvania.
Philadelphia Museum of Art, Philadelphia, Pennsylvania.
The Museums at Stony Brook, Stony Brook, New York.
Winchenton Historical Society, Winchenton, Massachusetts.

*Painted wooden swinging rocking horse made c. 1900.
(Margaret Woodbury Strong Museum, New York)*

*Shoofly, late 19th century with painted decorations, possibly Crandall (Essex
Institute, Salem)*

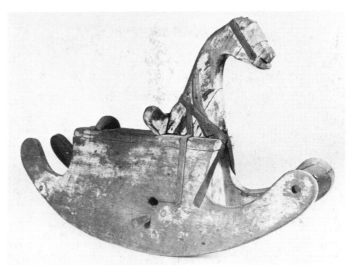

*Painted wooden horse, smoked with candles, c. 1820 (Bucks County Historical
Society, Doylestown)*

95

Bibliography

Rocking Horses

D'ALLEMAGNE, H.R.   *Histoire des Jouets & Récréations et Passetemps.* Hatchette, Paris, 1905.

DAIKEN, Leslie   *Children's Toys Throughout the Ages.* Batsford, London, 1952.

DEW, Anthony   *Rocking Horse Making.* David & Charles, Newton Abbott, 1984.

FAWDRY, K & M.   *Pollock's History of English Toys & Dolls.* Ernest Benn, London, 1979.

FLICK, Pauline   *Discovering Toys and Toy Museums.* Shire Publications, 1971.

FRASER, Antonia   *A History of Toys.* Weidenfeld & Nicholson, London, 1966.

Gamage's Christmas Bazaar 1913. Reprint David & Charles, Newton Abbott, 1974.

KING, Constance E.   *The Encyclopedia of Toys.* Robert Hale, London, 1978.

MAYHEW, Henry   *Articles in the 'Morning Chronicle' February 25th 1856.*

MURRAY, Patrick   *Toys.* Studio Vista, 1968.

McCLINTOCK, Marshall & Inez   *Toys in America.* Public Affairs Press, Washington, 1961.

WHITE, Gwen   *Antique Toys and Their Background.* Batsford, London, 1971.

Horses

RAYFIELD, Donald   *The Dream of Lhasa. The Life of Nikolay Przhevalsky.* Paul Elek, London, 1976.

TRENCH, Charles Chenevix   *A History of Horsemanship.* Longman, London, 1970.

TREW, Cecil G.   *The Accoutrements of the Riding Horse.* Seeley Service Co. London.

Roundabouts

BEAUVAU, Louis de   *Fête et Carrousel.* Crapelet, Paris, 1828.

BRAITHWAITE, David   *Fairground Architecture.* Hugh Evelyn, London, 1968.

BRAITHWAITE, David   *Savages of King's Lynn.* Patrick Stephens, Cambridge, 1975.

CHRISTENSON, Ervin   *Early American Wood Carving.* World Publishing Co., Cleveland, 1952.

CLARK, H. Ronald   *Savages Ltd.* Modern Press, Norwich, 1964.

FRIED, Frederick   *A Pictorial History of the Carousel.* A. S. Barnes & Co., New York, 1964.

HAMLIN, John   *Flying Horses, The Story of the Merry Go Round.* J. P. Lippincott, Philadelphia, USA, 1942.

HATCH-ALDEN   *'General Ike'.* Henry Holt & Co, USA.

HERZOG, Sybil Jean   *Round and Round.* New York Times Magazine, 1946.

JONES, Barbara   *The Unsophisticated Arts.* Architectural Press, London, 1951.

LAMBERT, Margaret & MARX, Enid   *English Popular Art.* Batsford, London, 1951.

LINES, Walter   *Looking Backwards & Looking Forwards.* Lines Brothers Ltd, Merton, 1958.

ROOPE, F. C.   *Come to the Fair.* The World's Fair, Oldham, 1962.

WARE, Michael E.   *Historic Fairground Scenes.* Moorland Publishing Co., Buxton, Derbyshire, 1977.

WEEDON, G. and WARD, R.   *Fairground Art.* White Mouse Editions, New Cavendish Press, 1981.

WHITE, Paul   *Fairs & Circus.* Adam & Charles Black, London, 1982.